MURDER & MAYHEM CUMBERLAND COUNTY

MURDER & MAYHEM CUMBERLAND COUNTY

JOSEPH DAVID CRESS

THE
History
PRESS

Published by The History Press
Charleston, SC 29403
www.historypress.net

All images courtesy of the Cumberland County Historical Society unless otherwise noted.

First published 2010

ISBN 978.1.59629.884.2

Cress, Joseph David.
Murder & mayhem in Cumberland County / Joseph David Cress.
p. cm.
Includes bibliographical references.
ISBN 9781540234896
1. Murder--Pennsylvania--Cumberland County--History--Case studies. 2. Violent crimes-
-Pennsylvania--Cumberland County--History--Case studies. I. Title. II. Title: Murder and
mayhem in Cumberland County.
HV6533.P4C74 2010
364.152'30974843--dc22
2010024022

Notice: The information in this book is true and complete to the best of our knowledge. It is offered without guarantee on the part of the author or The History Press. The author and The History Press disclaim all liability in connection with the use of this book.

CONTENTS

CONTENTS

ACKNOWLEDGEMENTS

First of all, I want to thank my wife, Stacey, along with our friends and family who continue to support me as I take my writing in a new and exciting direction. Your love has made it possible for me to fulfill a dream. I also dedicate this book to the memory of two souls who had a profound impact on my life.

My mother, Christina, encouraged me from an early age to pursue writing as both a passion and career. From her, I learned how to take a stand, question authority, dare to be different and persevere.

A dear friend, Bob Missimer, had the storytelling gift—the power to move you with just the sound of his voice. His was a creative soul taken from us too soon. From Bob, I learned to be confident and unafraid of what others may think of me. I learned that life is too short to sit and wonder how to make your dreams come true.

I also want to thank the dedicated and professional staff at the Cumberland County Historical Society (CCHS). They helped me immensely in the research that went into this project. Special thanks go out to the crew in the photo archives, who worked under a tight deadline to deliver the images found in this book.

My gratitude also goes out to the leadership team at the *Sentinel* newspaper and to the editorial staff at The History Press for all the opportunities you have given me over the years.

INTRODUCTION

E very community, large and small, has its share of black marks mixed in with a colorful past. These shady spots of tragedy and outrage, treachery and madness, have their own dark allure that can light our path to a greater understanding of the human condition.

Cumberland County in Pennsylvania is no different. Darkness always lingers beneath layers of civility, and when it shows itself, we are left both shocked and morbidly curious. We may not like what we see, but when we think about how fragile life is, some good may come out of this quiet reflection—something of the light may shine through for us.

When I set out on this path in October 2009, I wanted this book to be a mixture of murder and mayhem both high-profile and virtually unknown. I thought if I could lace my poison pen with such a wide variety of cases, I could draw the attention of readers new to local history and county historians in search of fresh insight. For this, my second book, I purchased some scary soundtracks in eager anticipation of spending hours in a dimly lit corner of my attic office enjoying the craft of writing. After weeks spent in research, the first chapter was written on Halloween. I thought, how appropriate.

You hold in your hands the product of six months of research and writing. There are twenty sections arranged chronologically under six thematic parts. Within these pages are the confessions of the condemned, the musings of poets, eyewitness testimony and media reports spanning more than 225 years of Cumberland County history, from the Pontiac War to the Camp Hill Prison Riots.

The *American Volunteer* newspaper was printed out of this office on South Bedford Street in Carlisle circa 1880s. The site is now occupied by the First Lutheran Church.

Brace yourself going forward. This is not for the meek or fainthearted. You will stare into the eyes of a murderer who changed courthouse security. You will see the faces of three sisters killed out of mercy and torment. You will read the words of a crazed alcoholic who thought that his wife could assist in his suicide—after she was dead. And you will meet two young sweethearts forever united in death by a single fatal bullet.

It has often been said that journalism is history in its first draft. After almost twenty years of being a reporter, I feel my age and wonder what history I have chronicled for future generations to draw from. Much of what follows is based on firsthand accounts by fellow journalists, many of whom had their names lost to history before bylines were a common newsroom practice.

This book is for them to show the public that there is value in newspapers even as the industry struggles to stay relevant and competitive in a noisy world crowded with demands for our attention. The hard work and dedication of these journalists made this history of murder and mayhem possible. It is my hope that you, the reader, will come to honor them and to learn from them as much as I have.

PART I

BLOOD FOR BLOOD

Terrorism is not a modern invention, nor is the blood feud. Cumberland County in the 1760s stretched beyond Pittsburgh and occupied much of southwestern Pennsylvania. The modern towns of Carlisle and Shippensburg were outposts on the edge of civilization and a sparsely populated wilderness. As settlers moved west, they encroached on native territory, setting the stage for mayhem and atrocities committed on both sides. The ferocity of the terror raids would cast the Indian as a brute deserving of conquest, while equally violent men among the colonists would escape justice. In between, women and children paid the price.

"The Greatest Melancholy": The Pontiac War

Terror stalked the hills and valleys beyond Carlisle. Months had passed since the Indian tribes unleashed the Conspiracy of Pontiac on unsuspecting settlers of what was then a vast Cumberland County. The attacks sprang out of lingering rage brought on by broken promises made by the British empire. Before it was over, the Pontiac War would leave behind a landscape virtually empty of colonists but full of death and devastation. The county seat of Carlisle had become an emergency refugee center.

Soon after his arrival in town, Reverend William Thomson wrote a letter dated July 18, 1763, to the Society for the Propagation of the Gospel. In it he described the desperate suffering of the people, along with his own frustration over not being able to safely work his circuit of churches. What made conditions even more deplorable was the stark reality of having no relief in sight from the ravages of what he called "the Heathen":

> The Indians have again made incursions upon our frontiers, killing, scalping and butchering all who are so unhappy as to fall into their hands. There are upwards of 1,500 plantations evacuated and people are daily crowding towards the interior parts of the province for refuge, leaving all they have to the spoil of a merciless, cruelly Bloodthirsty Barbarian…I have brought my wife to this town where every hut is filled with helpless women and children and where we expect almost every moment an invasion from our enemies…Every face here is covered with the greatest melancholy and despair.

When Colonel Henry Bouquet reached Carlisle that same month, he had hoped to find enough wagons and provisions to supply his army in its march west to relieve forts under siege by the Indians. The plan was to also muster recruits to fill out his companies and form additional militia units for the fight ahead. Instead, the Swiss mercenary found a community of refugees begging for food, medicine and protection. Bouquet felt obliged to distribute some food meant for his army to the half-starved civilians crowded into Fort Lowther and every other shelter in town. In a July 1 letter to Governor James Hamilton, Bouquet asked that reinforcements be sent immediately to Carlisle, along with stores of provisions, clothing, arms and equipment:

> The inhabitants in their present position, are utterly unable to defend their scattered plantations, and should they be so lucky as to reap their harvest, they have no means to save it from the flames…Their spirits are cast down at the dismal prospect of impending ruin and it is more than probable that they will desert the county on the first attack, which would be fatal to the province; as so many families crowding on the rest would spread a general panic and confusion.

To prevent this, Bouquet proposed a new defensive strategy, which he wrote "may appear hard on the people, but will be their safety in the end, if taken in time." Realizing the futility of trying to save all of Cumberland County, he suggested that parts of it be abandoned to the Indians and that seven or eight forts be developed at strategic locations near mills. These forts would provide a refuge for settlers, who would be directed to destroy what

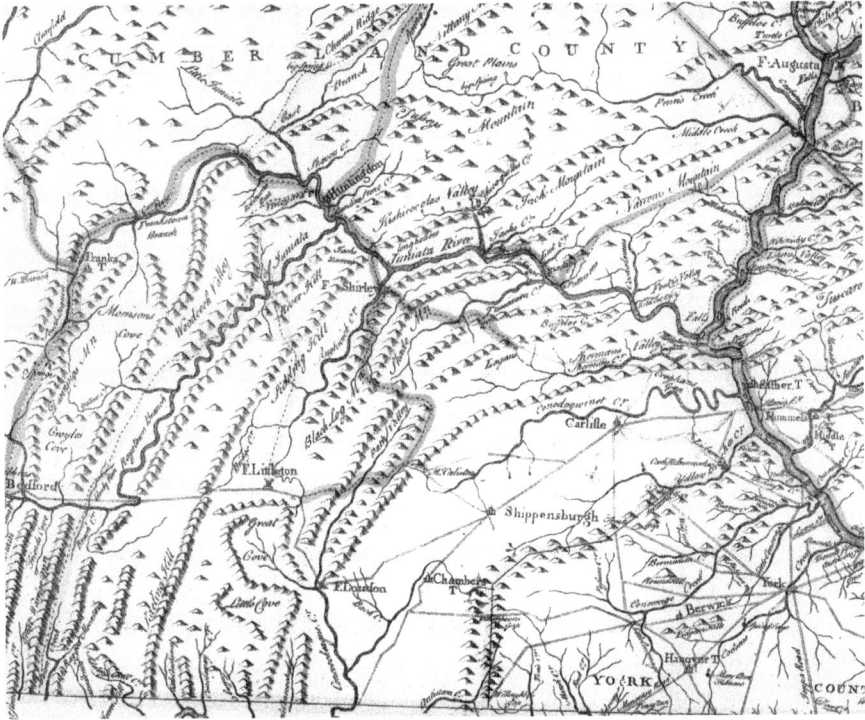

This map by W. Scull, circa 1770, shows part of the once vast Cumberland County.

provisions they could not carry in order to deprive the Indians of food and supplies. Bouquet also suggested that the government support the rationing of what supplies could be salvaged from the frontier.

Two weeks later, on July 13, 1763, Bouquet wrote to Hamilton that nineteen people had been killed within forty miles of Carlisle and that acts of violence by Indians were on the increase. As before, Bouquet made a plea for reinforcements saying that he could scarcely describe the horror of seeing "the desolation of so many families reduced to the last extremities of want and misery." Bouquet added that the whole country west of Carlisle is chiefly abandoned, along with the harvest, cattle and horses:

> *Finding myself unable…to afford any direction to this frontier, I thought it incumbent…to recommend it to your immediate protection; as it was easy to judge from the general panic and the dispersion of the inhabitants that a handful of savages would soon lay waste the country…I march the day after tomorrow to the relief of Fort Pitt, and hope to draw the attention of the enemy upon me.*

While in Carlisle, Bouquet received a message from British general John Amherst urging him to use whatever means possible to destroy the enemy. One suggestion that the general made was to find a way to spread smallpox among the hostile tribes. Bouquet advised Amherst that he would try and get a supply of blankets to pox victims at Fort Pitt and then use friendly Indians to distribute the infested blankets to the enemy tribes. While there is no direct evidence to suggest that this plan was actually carried out, the Ohio tribes did suffer an epidemic of the disease two months after Amherst made his request.

Meanwhile, Bouquet was able to secure wagons and packhorses from Lancaster and York Counties for the relief convoy to Fort Pitt. In mid-July, Bouquet marched out of Carlisle with two companies of Royal American colonial troops, five hundred Highlanders, thirty experienced woodsmen and rangers from Lancaster and Cumberland Counties. Many Highland soldiers were sick with a fever they contracted while in the West Indies prior to coming to Pennsylvania.

The expedition arrived in Ligonier by July 28 and first made contact with Pontiac's warriors in early August. The Battle of Bushy Run raged on for two days, resulting in a defeat for the Indians, who were forced to retreat out of the Fort Pitt region and back into the Ohio Valley.

Not much had changed from mid-July to early October when Thomson again wrote to the Gospel society. His letter makes references to the

Early engraving of Henry Bouquet.

successful campaign by Bouquet to relieve the "poor distressed people at Fort Pitt" trapped there for more than two months with inadequate provisions. Thomson mentioned the victory at Bushy Run but went on to write how Carlisle and the surrounding countryside were still subjected to the same level of terrorism:

> *Everything here is in the greatest confusion and utmost disorder. The farmers and inhabitants of this country are daily flying from place to place where they can have any prospect of safety...Many are reduced to...taking up their lodging in the open air without shelter or clothing to cover them from...the weather or even food for themselves or families to subsist on. Our ears are daily alarmed with the shocking news of fresh butcheries committed by the Heathen on some of our friends or neighbors.*

Thomson reported having difficulty visiting all his churches, but he also saw hope in the attitude of his parishioners. He described them as having "hearts glowing with the love of their country and religion" and the resolve to defend what is dear to them.

The plight of the refugees made such an impression on the people of eastern Pennsylvania that large donations were sent westward for them to

This engraving of the Square in Carlisle is adapted from Sherman Day's 1843 *Historical Collections of the State of Pennsylvania.*

15

purchase flour, rice and medicine. Displaced settlers also used the money to buy weapons and ammunition to use in defense upon return to their homes. It was a troubling time for the refugees in Carlisle, who often gathered on the Square in the evenings to listen to soldiers and travelers spin frontier tales.

The first seeds of conspiracy were planted after Brigadier General John Forbes took possession of Fort Duquesne in November 1758. This effectively put an end to a previous terror campaign perpetrated by the French and their Indian allies against the settlers of Cumberland County. It was understood by friendly tribes that the British would retreat back over the mountains once they had secured the frontier from further incursions by hostile forces, but that didn't happen.

Instead, the British not only reneged on their promise to withdraw their army from Indian territory, they also rebuilt Fort Duquesne—renaming it Fort Pitt—and reinforced other frontier outposts. A settlement began to grow around Fort Pitt. When the Indians complained, the British assured them that the beefed up defenses were not for occupation but rather for added security against the French and lawlessness on the frontier.

The British were also negotiating the permanent possession of the Ohio River Valley. It was agreed by treaty that the French would cede all of the territory they had occupied in Canada along with the areas around the Great Lakes and the Ohio River. This was done in defiance of Indian rights to the land and of promises made when the British were seeking aid from friendly tribes to expel the French. As early as 1759, tribal leaders began to mistrust the British, laying the groundwork for the Conspiracy of Pontiac.

Indian chiefs met repeatedly with leaders of the provincial government to protest the continued presence of settlers in their territory. The tribes warned the colonists that they would not tolerate this ongoing breach of faith, but these threats were ignored. Soon Pontiac, chief of the Ottawa tribe, emerged as a leader persuasive enough to unite the western tribes into a campaign to exterminate all settlers west of the mountains and to drive the colonists back into the sea.

War chiefs ordered braves to visit the trading houses of Fort Pitt and other frontier outposts to buy more lead, powder, knives, guns and hatchets instead of the gaudy trinkets and other goods the traders had for sale. These purchases went unnoticed by settlers, who carried on the routine of peace, unaware of the gathering conspiracy on the horizon that had set the end of May 1763 as the launch date. The goal was to kill without mercy every soldier, trader and settler on the frontier in one swift terror campaign. Stories of murder and mayhem persisted well into 1764 as the Indian raids hit even closer to home.

On March 19, 1764, Indians killed a man and took five prisoners from the Letterkenny area where, three days later, seven homes were destroyed by fire. In the ensuing panic, several Shippensburg-area families fled, including one with a woman who had just given birth two hours before her forced departure.

In late July, Thomas Pomeroy returned to his Lurgen Township home after a hunting trip only to find his entire family murdered by Indians. The sole survivor from the household was a neighbor named Mrs. Johnston, who was visiting Pomeroy's wife and two children at the time. Alive but suffering from a fractured skull and broken arm, Johnston was taken to Shippensburg but died within hours of her arrival.

The threat of Indian raids prompted settlers in the Juniata and Cumberland Valleys to flee south and east toward Carlisle, York and Lancaster. Nearly 1,400 refugees had crowded into Shippensburg, which lies west of Carlisle and was the original county seat.

Word of the atrocities spread all the way to Philadelphia, where the *Pennsylvania Gazette* reported on the death of a seventeen-year-old girl killed near Big Spring as she was returning home from church. A daughter of James Dyhart, she was murdered, scalped and left naked by the Indians. In its August 9, 1764 edition, the *Gazette* reported how a pregnant woman named Cunningham was found dead about two miles south of Fort Loudon in present-day Fulton County. The newspaper described how she was attacked by Indians, who killed and scalped her before cutting the baby out of her body and leaving it beside her.

The violence would eventually end between the settlers and native tribes, only to move westward with the advance of the ideal of Manifest Destiny. Over time, Cumberland County shrank in size as other counties splintered off from what was once an untamed frontier. But even today, there are lingering signs of past outrage committed by both sides, including a monument to a schoolhouse massacre.

"A Perfect Holocaust": The Enoch Brown Massacre

Little Archie McCullough was blind and among the ten lifeless bodies sprawled on the blood-soaked floor of the log schoolhouse. A horrified settler, first on the scene, watched the boy crawl among the dead using his hands to smooth over the faces and run his fingers through their hair.

It was as if the sole survivor was trying to distinguish by touch one slain classmate from the next. The whole time, the ten-year-old boy moaned in pain from trauma he suffered after an Indian raider clubbed him on the head before taking away part of his scalp. Though McCullough recovered from his wounds and lived to old age, his mind was never the same after the massacre of July 25, 1764. The uncanny silence of the dead schoolhouse, located three miles northwest of Greencastle, drew the curiosity of the passing settler.

There were hints of foreboding on the morning of the tragedy. Local resident Richard Bard would later recall how his father, working near the school, noticed that the family dog was behaving strangely. Convinced that there were Indians sneaking through a nearby thicket, the father returned home to safety. Legend has it that several students, who normally enjoyed school, refused to go that day and so stayed home and survived. One boy, after leaving home, decided that he would not go to school but rather would wander through the woods. Hot weather combined with seasonal chores at home kept other students from attending school.

The morning started innocently enough. Schoolmaster Enoch Brown arrived early to prepare for the day as the students trickled in. Within an hour of opening the building, Brown told the students to settle down. He called roll, but only eight boys and two girls responded. McCullough was the youngest student that day, while Eben Taylor was the oldest at age fifteen. The record identifies a third boy as George Dunstan and the girls as Ruth Hart and Ruth Hale. The other names are lost to history.

McCullough would report how two boys told Brown that they saw Indians in the bushes on their way to school. Having heard of past rumors of alleged native activity, the teacher dismissed the warning as the product of their vivid imagination. Brown went on with the lesson plan. Shortly after opening exercises, there came a noise at the door, which drew the attention of Brown. He was shocked to see the door thrown open by three Indians, who stood at the threshold blocking the exit.

History describes Brown as a kindhearted man respected in the community for his integrity, honesty and Christian character. Realizing that there was no escape, it was reported that Brown stepped up to the door and pleaded with the Indians to spare the children. The book *The History of Franklin County* had this commentary on what happened next: "The teacher offered his life and scalp in a spirit of self-sacrificing devotion…But no! the tender mercies of the heathen are cruel, and so a perfect holocaust was made to the Moloch of war by the relentless fiends in human form."

One Indian told Brown that they would have to kill all of the children to avoid detection and escape. He sprang forward through the door and attacked the teacher with a wooden mallet. Brown tried to use his hands to defend himself, but soon they were battered and broken, and heavy blows soon struck Brown on the head, causing the teacher to fall to the floor dying.

As the Indian murdered Brown, the children panicked and started to run around the inside of the schoolhouse. The two Indians outside prevented the students from escaping into the underbrush around the crude log structure. They also guided the first Indian to each child. One by one, the students were killed by blows from the heavy mallet until nine little corpses joined Brown on the schoolhouse floor. With no time to lose, the murderer went from one body to the next, cutting away their scalps with a knife.

Somehow, amid the confusion, Archie McCullough managed to hide himself behind some dried branches in the fireplace. From that vantage point, he witnessed the slaughter of his schoolmates and avoided the attention of the Indians. But looking back, the murderer saw McCullough and came rushing at him, hitting him once with the mallet. The boy was left for dead and the Indians escaped.

The schoolhouse was located on a cleared field at the end of a deep ravine surrounded by dense forest. It is believed that the Indians went down the ravine to the Conococheague Creek, where they then used the water to conceal their tracks to the mouth of the Path Valley and across the mountains. In his book, *A History of the Cumberland Valley*, Dr. George P. Donehoo mentioned how Bard's father saw a group of settlers pursue what could have been the same Indians involved in the massacre.

The accounts vary on the age of the perpetrators. Archie McCullough said that the Indians outside were older than the Indian inside the school who did all the killing. His cousin, John McCullough, was captured by the natives exactly eight years before the massacre at a location a few miles southwest of the log schoolhouse. The cousin became the adopted son of Delaware Indians, who had retreated to the shores of the Muskingum on the upper Ohio River soon after 1758.

In his narrative, John McCullough explained how more than three hundred Indians had gathered on the Forks of the Muskingum to raid settlements but that this large attack was abandoned for unspecified reasons. However, smaller parties of warriors did go out and raid settlements, including the three Indians involved in the schoolhouse massacre. The cousin said that he was well acquainted with the raiders and described them as "young fellows, perhaps none…more than 20 years of age."

Tribal elders, including an old chief named Night Walker, disapproved of the killing of so many children and publicly denounced the three raiders as cowards. Donehoo wrote, "The entire incident is more in keeping with the actions of young warriors, anxious to get scalps, than of old warriors, seeking revenge upon their enemies. Many of the worst and most savage acts of cruelty during the period of these frontier raids, were committed, according to the statements of the old warriors, by young men."

Sources vary on the background of the murdered children. Some say that each student belonged to a different family, while the *Pennsylvania Gazette* reported how two of the children belonged to "an unhappy man" who had four other children carried off by savages during the last Indian war. The *Gazette*, in its initial story of the massacre, reported how one boy survived only to later die of injuries. In a follow-up story, the newspaper corrected itself, noting that the unnamed boy (probably Archie McCullough) was alive. The teacher along with his students were placed in a large wooden box and buried in a common grave.

White settlers were guilty of their own atrocities, including several triggered by the passage of the Scalp Act in April 1756. This new law offered a bounty of about $130 for the scalp of any Indian male over ten years old and $50 for the scalp of any Indian woman. This encouraged settlers to send out war parties into native territory to kill and scalp hostile Indians. The act also offered cash rewards for the delivery of any captured Indians to frontier forts or towns.

This measure was opposed by Conrad Weiser and other Indian traders, who argued that there was no way of telling the difference between the scalp of a hostile Indian and that of a friendly Indian. They also felt that the Scalp Act would be a barrier to lasting peace and would only lead to more tension on the frontier.

Sure enough, many friendly Indians, including women and children, were killed so that greedy colonists could collect the scalp bounty. There were even cases of white men marrying Indian women just so they could kill and scalp their own children for the Crown to pay the blood money.

Other atrocities committed by settlers had more to do with pure hatred, bigotry and vendetta. In January 1768—almost four years after the Enoch Brown Massacre—ten local Indians from a friendly tribe were killed in a massacre of innocence perpetrated by two white settlers who ultimately escaped justice.

The Indians had visited a cabin on Middle Creek north of Carlisle to ask its occupants, Frederick Stump and John Ironcutter, for food or work. Drunk at the time, Stump fought with the Indians, and in the struggle that followed, he and Ironcutter murdered four men and two women. The rest escaped. The killers cut holes in the ice of a nearby creek to conceal the bodies.

The next day, Stump and Ironcutter traveled to an Indian cabin about fourteen miles up the creek and killed an Indian woman and three children before setting the cabin on fire. News of the murders spread rapidly, along with the fear that the brutal slayings could spark the need for revenge among the Indians and reignite open conflict on the frontier. Civil authorities pushed to have the murderers arrested so as to preserve the peace throughout Cumberland County. Both were apprehended and held in Carlisle, where they escaped after a group of armed men stormed the county jail to force their release. It is said Stump and Ironcutter were never seen nor heard from again by the authorities despite attempts to find them.

Seventy-nine years later, on August 4, 1843, Greencastle-area residents excavated the remains of the Enoch Brown Massacre victims to verify the place and manner of burial. They unearthed fragments of a roughly made coffin, the skull and bones of a grown person and the skeletal remains of several children. Other relics found included metal buttons, pieces of a tobacco box and teeth. The bodies were reburied.

The common grave marker of Enoch Brown and his students.

For years, local residents pushed for a monument at the site, but this proposal only received serious consideration in 1885 when a spirited capital campaign raised about $1,400 from local schools. Organizers purchased twenty acres and commissioned a monument, which was unveiled before a crowd of about five thousand people on August 4, 1885. Four girls and nine boys pulled the chords on the red, white and blue mantle that covered the monument.

An engraving on its north side notes that the monument was erected at the direction of the Franklin County Centennial Convention of April 22, 1884, in the name of the teachers and scholars of all the schools in the county. The west-side inscription nearest the grave mentions how Enoch Brown and his students "fell as pioneer martyrs in the cause of education and Christian civilization." On the east side is a dedication to their memory, while on the south side there is the following poem:

> *The ground is holy where they fell,*
> *And where their mingled ashes lie,*
> *Ye Christian people, mark it well*
> *With granite columns strong and high;*
> *And cherish well forevermore*
> *The storied wealth of early years,*
> *The sacred legacies of yore,*
> *The toils and trials of pioneers.*

Dr. Cyrus Cort, who spoke at the dedication, mentioned the fate of Elenore Cochran, Mary Ramsey and Sarah Brown, three students not present on the day of the massacre. Cochran had a granddaughter who married General Stonewall Jackson. Ramsey was great-aunt to Jane and Elizabeth Irvin who married sons of President William H. Harrison. Brown became the mother of George Chambers, a future congressman and state Supreme Court justice.

PART II

SUFFER THE CHILDREN

S ome of the most horrific crimes are committed against children. What motivates anyone to slaughter innocence can be as varied as any mass murder, but the chapters that follow have a common thread of madness. The first is the story of a spiteful youth in bondage looking for any means to escape the lash. The third is a tale of a desperate father who would rather see his offspring destroyed than suffer through the torture of starvation. In between, there is a total mystery that left a family destroyed and a community shocked by the methodical skill of its execution.

"THE FIERCE INDIGNATION OF HEAVEN": TEEN SLAVE CHILD KILLER

Her hand clamped down on the mouth of the child, Chloe could feel the dying breath of four-year-old Lucetta Carothers. It was Saturday, January 24, 1801, and the teenage slave had invited the little girl to accompany her on chores along the creek that ran through a nearby meadow. In her confession printed in the *Carlisle Gazette*, Chloe claimed that she intended no harm to Lucetta at first but later felt tempted to kill the child out of revenge toward the girl's mother: "I immediately laid hold of her, and laid my hand on her mouth, and held it as long as I could perceive any breath; then threw her into the run; took home the water, and entirely forgot what I had done, until about an hour later."

It was about 3:00 p.m. when Mary Carothers noticed that her daughter was missing, after her husband, Andrew, had asked where Lucetta was. The family launched a search as chronicled in the confession, supposedly taken directly from the lips of Chloe by a Methodist clergyman on the eve of her July 18, 1801 execution: "My master call[ed] to me [wanting] to know if Lucetta was with me. I answered no. This was the first of my recollecting what I had done…My master found her in the run. As yet, I believe there was no suspicion of my being the murderer. I now promised myself good days, at least so long as my mistress's trouble lasted; but I found it otherwise."

In her journal article, "Chloe's Story," Nancy Lougridge provided details on the background of this teenage slave turned child killer. She wrote how, on March 31, 1789, William Kelso of East Pennsboro Township traveled from Lemoyne to the county seat of Carlisle to register the birth of Chloe as December 1782. A wealthy innkeeper, Kelso owned a ferry crossing over the Susquehanna River. In her confession, Chloe mentioned how Kelso died when she was young and that she was willed to his daughter, Rebecca.

The next mention of Chloe was of her being sold to Philadelphia slave dealer John W. Godfrey on July 4, 1794. What followed was a four-month period in which the eleven-year-old slave girl had five different masters, but no one knows why. There is speculation by Lougridge that Chloe may have been emotionally unstable, mentally retarded or so brutalized over the years that her rage was unmanageable.

In March 1795, Chloe was sold to Oliver Pollock, a wealthy merchant and financier who maintained homes in both Cumberland County and Philadelphia. Chloe stayed in the Pollock household for almost two years before being sold to Andrew Carothers on November 21, 1796.

Carothers was described as a hardworking, frugal man whose wife, Mary, needed help with cooking and household chores. The couple had six children and lived together in a one-room cabin. Where Chloe slept is unknown, but clearly there was tension in the household, as evidenced by her confession of lost faith and ever growing violent thoughts: "While I lived with Mr. Pollock, I was taught my prayers and other duties by his youngest daughter. But to my grief, I seldom said them; and when I did, it was in a very indifferent and cold manner. At the same time, I was much addicted to vice though never guilty of stealing or lying."

Instead, Chloe said that her vice was foul language, a crime she thought would go unpunished in her mortal life but one she would answer to in the afterlife. The slave also admitted a desire for revenge for her ill treatment over the years. Aside from murder, Chloe confessed to trying to burn down

The Oliver Pollock House in Silver Spring Township.

the Carothers family barn and to contemplating harming the couple's youngest son.

From the beginning, Mary Carothers suspected Chloe of murdering Lucetta. She was convinced that her youngest daughter could have crawled out of the creek on her hands and feet unless someone held the girl down. When confronted with this theory, Chloe denied any involvement even after being subjected to beatings, as described in her confession: "The funeral was scarcely over, being on Sunday, when she [Mary Carothers] made me strip off my short gown and gave me a severe whipping with a cow skin; also on Tuesday she gave me another; and on the following Saturday she gave me a third."

The mother, who was so determined to beat a confession out of the slave girl, only set the stage for further tragedy. Bent on revenge, Chloe convinced six-year-old Polly to accompany her to the creek a week after Lucetta died. In her own words, Chloe explained what happened next: "When there, I asked her why she told everything upon me? She answered her mother desired her to do so. I said you shall never tell anymore on me. I then laid hold of her, and…laid my hand on her mouth, and held it near the space of half an hour, then I threw her into the run. I remained secure in my mind without any fear or distress."

About noon on January 31, 1801, Chloe was ordered to fetch some sandstone and a kettle of water from the creek to scrub the cabin floor. Meanwhile, Polly was instructed to find a basin to use to spread sand on the floor. Mary Carothers first noticed her daughter missing when she needed help to move furniture so that Chloe could scrub the floor. The six-year-old was later found dead near where Lucetta had died just the week before. Mary Carothers would testify how Chloe came running up with the news, wringing her hands and pretending to cry. "The body had not lain near so long in the water," Mary Carothers said of Polly. "The body was not near so cold as the first."

Ever more suspicious, the mother resumed the beatings; while she could barely tolerate the sight of Chloe, Mary Carothers could not secure a confession from the slave girl. At one point, she promised to spare Chloe from the gallows and instead sell her back to Philadelphia, but Chloe refused to cooperate. It was no doubt frustrating. Finally, a neighbor named John Clendenin persuaded Chloe to confess to the double murder and face the consequences. Chloe explained what happened in her confession: "The horrors of a guilty conscience awoke within me. I was much whipped by my master to extort a confession, but I was much more lashed by my own conscience." Her motive was also reported in her published confession:

> *The reason why I killed them, was not because I had any spite or malice against them. On the contrary, I loved them both…I knew that the children were compelled by my mistress to give information respecting some parts of my conduct; for which I was severely corrected, far beyond the demerit of the fault. To cut off this means of information, was the first end I promised myself. But my second and greatest motive was to bring all the misery I possibly could upon the family and particularly upon my mistress…The desire of revenge plunged me into that greatest of all crimes—the murder of two innocent children.*

John Clendenin escorted Chloe to the county jail in Carlisle, where she was charged with first-degree murder. Her trial was held that June, with Mary Carothers giving most of the testimony. In her article, Lougridge wrote how neither Andrew Carothers nor Chloe were called to the stand.

It is unknown whether anyone spoke on Chloe's behalf, but the slave girl probably didn't have a defense attorney. Objections were raised but later thrown out against the death penalty. Lougridge wrote how it was unclear who raised the objections or what they were, but one must have been that Chloe was incompetent and not responsible for her actions.

A death warrant was later issued to John Carothers, Cumberland County sheriff and Andrew's cousin. That Chloe felt remorse is apparent in her confession, along with her judging the worthiness of her soul on the eve of her execution:

> *Oh, what have I done? In revenging the injuries I suffered, I have drawn the fierce indignation of Heaven upon myself...Is my sin too great for the mercy of God to pardon? Is my stain too deep for the Blood of Jesus to wash away? I am still encouraged to trust. Loud as the blood of these innocents cries for vengeance, the Blood of Jesus cries louder still for mercy and pardon; and I trust that His unbounded goodness will not suffer me to perish.*

"WHAT...FIENDISH CAUSE": THE BRUSHTOWN TRAGEDY

One can read into any face a natural gut reaction and pass judgment on guilt or innocence. A newspaper reporter, his name lost to history, came to the funeral hoping somehow to find the answer to the most basic question. Like so many others that June 1883, he struggled to understand why this mother of three would suddenly slit the throats of her children before taking her own life. He gazed down upon the bodies and later wrote the following for the *American Volunteer*:

> *Her features were natural but a look into that face did not arouse the same emotion in the heart that a look upon the faces of the children did. It was not love or pity or grief. It was rather a feeling of horror possibly resentment...The eye instinctively searched for marks of the demon or traces of insanity in those dead features. Neither could be discerned and when you turned away your mind was as much mystified.*

There was no mistaking that the three raven-haired boys were brothers. It was reported how shrouds covered the cruel gash in each tiny throat and

27

how the little hands were crossed and in them were placed bunches of roses and other seasonal flowers. A reporter with the *Carlisle Herald* had this to say: "The face of each victim was a picture of beauty and intelligence that all who beheld them will remember to their dying day and wonder what mysterious or fiendish cause could compel a mother to take the lives of such sweet and innocent babes. Human comprehension staggers under the effort."

There were theories on a possible motive. The *Carlisle Herald* reported how a rumor circulated that, about five months before the tragedy, the family physician told Mrs. Daniel Vance that her daughter, Susan Dessie Douglas, showed signs of insanity and needed extra supervision. Dr. H.H. Longsdorf said that Douglas, while pregnant with her youngest son, developed symptoms of Bright's disease of the kidney and a "consequent softening of the brain."

Both newspapers reported how Douglas was upset about rumors circulating through the neighborhood of Brushtown about her chastity and character. The *Carlisle Herald* had this to say: "It preyed upon her mind and it is said that once, when her husband was about leaving home to go to work she, in a very positive manner, declared to him that she could not stand these ugly reports about her. He spoke to her kindly and begged her not

Dr. Harold Hamilton Longsdorf, circa 1923.

to mind them and said that all would be well, but she refused to be consoled and an awful crime followed."

The *American Volunteer* speculated that "the busy tongue of scandal" combined with her own "morbid sensibility" compelled Douglas to take a straight razor from the top drawer of her husband's bureau and begin to cut throats. Before she was done, Douglas had killed all three of her sons and slashed her own throat six to eight times, almost severing the head from the body.

Up until that time, Brushtown was a quiet collection of log structures scattered along a section of road between Doubling Gap and Pine Grove in Penn Township about eleven miles southwest of Carlisle. There were not enough buildings to call it a village. A United Brethren church and a store stood near the center of the neighborhood, and a stone schoolhouse was located just down the road. Many of the inhabitants worked the land for local farmers or were employed at the furnace and ore mines at Pine Grove or Laurel Run.

The *American Volunteer* describes Susan Dessie Douglas as a strong-willed woman who "had her way in everything." Industrious, she took good care of her home and children but was not frugal or economical. There were no reports of fighting with her husband, Martin Douglas, described as a quiet, inoffensive man of lithe frame and medium height. A likeable fellow, he worked the ore banks at Pine Grove, providing well for his family. The couple had been married for about five years.

Typically, Martin Douglas left for work either on Sunday evenings or Monday mornings and returned again late on Saturday to spend Sundays with his family. On occasion, he would visit home midway through the week to deliver groceries before heading off again to work the next day.

Everything seemed fine when Martin Douglas kissed his children, said goodbye and promised to bring them new shoes when he returned from work. The following day, Mrs. Vance visited her daughter and stayed there until about 9:00 p.m., when all three children were asleep in bed. When Vance left, her daughter was in good spirits, and there was no reason to suspect that the children were in mortal danger.

The next morning, Vance peered out from her doorway and noticed an unusual silence brooding over her daughter's home just across the road, only forty steps away. She suspected that something was wrong, so she went over to investigate. Vance tried the front door but found it was locked. She then rapped on the front window of the bedroom, which was right where her daughter and three grandchildren slept. No response. She rapped again, even harder, but still there was dead silence. The *American Volunteer* reported what happened next:

> *Her heart began to flutter and a strange dread began to creep over her. She feared something terrible had happened and she hurried around to the door of the summer kitchen which she found unlocked. She opened it and entered and from the summer kitchen entered the kitchen, that door also being unbolted. She hurried through to the bed chamber, pushed open the door and there lay her daughter stone dead with her throat cut through to the spinal column. It was a sickening sight for a stout-hearted man to come upon, it was a thousand times worse for a tender mother to thus discover the daughter whom twelve hours before she had left in good health and cheerful spirits.*

Then Vance saw her three grandsons, stiff and cold in the bed. George Edgar, barely five, was lying on his back and must have died without a struggle. In the middle, three-year-old William Franklin was partly turned over on his face, his right hand up slightly and fingers cut in what was perhaps a defensive wound. Next to the wall was Harry Albert, an infant barely three months old. There was a splash of blood on the wall. All three children had died from a single deep cut to the throat. The *American Volunteer* had this to say about the killings: "Reader, here stop and reflect on the enormity of the crime we have introduced to you and fathom, if you can, the feelings of the mother [Mrs. Vance] who found this wholesale butchery of her offspring... The hand that did it must have been nerved with devilish desperation."

The murders shocked the neighborhood as the news spread far and wide, eventually reaching the ears of Martin Douglas and Daniel Vance. "The sad affair cast a gloom over the whole community," the *Carlisle Herald* reported. "From the time the inquest was held until the bodies were taken away to their graves there was one constant stream of people to the scene to inform themselves of the facts and to see the victims," the *American Volunteer* reported.

The house was shut up with the undisturbed bodies until Abram Null, the local justice of the peace, could convene a coroner's inquest. Investigators went inside to view the crime scene. They noticed how Susan Douglas was lying on the floor in front and diagonal to the bed. Her hair was neatly combed and pulled into a bun on the back of her head. Her right arm lay extended, and about a foot from her hand was the bloodstained razor. Her feet extended under the bed and her shoes were off.

To them, it appeared that she had made her way quietly to the bed, murdered her children and then either sat or lay down on the floor to take her own life. They noticed how the gashes in her throat were the deepest near her chest but grew shallower near the chin, as though her strength was failing her. She was dressed in the same clothes she wore that Thursday.

Susan Douglas, along with her three sons, were laid in separate coffins and lined up lengthwise in front of the pulpit. Local newspapers reported between 1,200 and 1,500 attended the funeral at the Dunker Church in nearby Huntsdale. The *American Volunteer* reported how the church sanctuary was packed, while the *Carlisle Herald* reported that "fully one half of the crowd could not gain admittance."

Seeking solace, the congregation listened as the minister preached how this awful crime made a powerful argument against a sinner's dangerous course. "His words burned themselves into the hearts of many a hearer," the *American Volunteer* reported.

When the service was over, "a throng of sad faced people filed slowly through the church past the coffins to take a view of the victims," the *Carlisle Herald* reporter wrote.

The *American Volunteer* reporter described the scene:

> *When all had viewed the corpses, the coffins were closed, taken into the graveyard and lowered into one large grave…The air was damp and chilly, the skies, which had been overcast all morning, commenced misting and then raining as if nature had been overcome and was shedding tears over the sad occasion.*

"A Soft Tish, Tish, Tish": The Babes in the Woods Mystery

No one could believe that the police were letting civilians view the bodies. Word spread quickly through the streets of Carlisle and beyond. Within half an hour, the sidewalk in front of Ewing's Funeral Home on South Hanover Street was densely packed with people both morbidly curious and genuinely concerned. The hope was someone within this crowd would recognize the pale, death-swollen faces of three little sisters dressed in white linen and laid out on gurneys in the county morgue. Any clue would have been welcome in the Babes in the Woods mystery.

State Trooper William Kaspervitch looked on as this procession of fascinated and horrified people filed past each corpse, stealing glances of the dead. Every so often, he would ask, "Do any of you recognize them?"

A line of people wait to enter the former Ewing Funeral Home at 148 South Hanover Street in Carlisle to view the bodies of the Babes in the Woods.

but there was never a reply to this most basic question. A *Sentinel* reporter stood by and observed that "the line moved with a silence peculiar to such occasions. No one was permitted to tarry. No one talked but many heads shook sadly and occasionally there was an 'ah' or a soft 'tish, tish, tish'…Mothers carried infants in their arms and clasped them tightly as they gazed upon the lifeless forms."

Police closed off access twice—first to fingerprint the children and then to give residents living above the funeral home relief from the crowd. An estimated ten thousand people had viewed the bodies in the twenty-four hours since the sisters were found dead near the edge of South Mountain about two miles north of Pine Grove Furnace. Yet no one, not a single soul, knew who they were or where they came from.

It all began at about 8:00 a.m. on Saturday, November 24, 1934, as John Clark and Clark Jardine went up into the mountain to cut wood. They came to a spot about twenty feet off South Mountain Road, which linked Pine Grove Furnace with Centerville. In a *Sentinel* article, John Clark recalled the grim discovery, thinking at first that it was either an illegal deer kill or an intoxicated worker:

We were figuring on which way to fell the tree when I seen the large blanket covering something large. Now right off when I see'd it I figured someone had shot a deer and…had just dropped it right there and ran. Then I saw a couple of beer bottles on the ground close by. Knowing there was a CCC [Civilian Conservation Corps] camp close in the vicinity, I figured someone from the camp had gotten full…and laid down to sleep it off. Then curiosity got the better of me and I went up to look under the corner of the blanket…First off, I thought there was just one body but Clark says "Uncle Jack, there's three bodies under that blanket"…But we didn't take any look any closer and hurried to the truck to get back to Huntsdale.

The men notified the police. Reporters from the *Sentinel* arrived on the scene before the district attorney and county coroner, only to find three girls lying dead between two green blankets. Each victim had light brown hair, freckles and gray eyes, leading witnesses to conclude that they were sisters. The bodies were laid side by side facing the same way, the arms of each sister over the body of the one next to her, almost in a posture of sleep. The top blanket covering them was only slightly wet, indicating to investigators they were placed in the woods the prior night just before an autumn rain had stopped falling at 9:30 p.m.

There were no signs of identification. The oldest and youngest child wore green coats and brown shoes, while the middle child wore a blue coat and black shoes. The oldest and youngest also had blood around their mouths. Each coat had a fur collar, and each girl was wearing an inexpensive but good-quality dress. Investigators set their ages at about eight, ten and thirteen years old.

Word spread rapidly across South Mountain and beyond. Hundreds of people rushed to the scene and were allowed to view the bodies before they were taken away. Many came looking for missing loved ones only to leave the scene disappointed. The sisters arrived in Carlisle at about 2:30 p.m. on Saturday and were taken to the funeral home, which served as the headquarters of an investigation that eventually involved twenty-eight states and captured front-page headlines nationwide.

Newspapers declared "Babes in the Woods" to be the biggest crime mystery since the Lindbergh baby kidnapping and murder—the trial of which began only five weeks after the girls were found. Star reporters were dispatched from all press associations and almost every major daily newspaper within three hundred miles of Carlisle. Press photographers shot hundreds of photos of the sisters, their clothing and the wooded area in which their bodies were found.

Aerial photos of South Mountain and Carlisle were taken by the score from low-flying planes. Police would distribute nearly three thousand photographs of the victims during the course of their intensive weeklong investigation.

Demand was so high for the latest news that Western Union and Post Telegraphy installed new circuits and Morse lines doubled the operating staff to provide twenty-four-hour service. Special wires were installed in a room at the Argonne Hotel where the press had set up its headquarters.

Roger H. Steck, city editor for the *Sentinel*, never saw such an influx of urban talent come into Carlisle to attend the daily news conferences. As investigators slowly pieced together the identity of the children and a theory on how they died, Steck could draw only one conclusion: "Some people don't get very good breaks in life." Reporter James R. Gouffer recalled the bedlam within the funeral home as calls came in from all over the country from fellow journalists. When not answering the phone or sleeping on the funeral home floor, Gouffer worked as a correspondent for the Associated Press and *Harrisburg Telegraph* newspaper.

The tragedy of the three sisters touched the hearts of local residents, who became protective of their mortal remains. American Legion Post 101 of Carlisle organized an effort to raise money for a modest funeral and the purchase of a burial plot. Post Commander David Binkley, who had three daughters of similar age to the victims, suggested the idea. "The death of these children in the bloom of happy girlhood is sad enough," Binkley told reporters. "Their burial in a potter's field and without benefit of proper religious rites would be a poor reflection on the community."

The Central Book Store on West High Street was set up as the collection point. The *Sentinel* reported how a young boy and his sister emptied their penny banks to donate fifty cents each to the fund but refused to give the reporter their names. The newspaper also reported how, on the afternoon of November 28, Donald and Helen Meals visited the funeral home and placed flowers besides the bodies of the little girls. The siblings vowed to bring fresh flowers each day until the sisters were laid to rest.

Two days later, on November 30, the *Sentinel* published a poem entitled "To the Memory of Three Little Girls" and written by a local resident with the initials M.A.E. The poem read in part:

> We thank Thee for a few small years
> Of life and childhood, smiles and tears;
> We thank Thee for the warm, soft earth.
> The kindest bed we've known since birth.

Suffer the Children

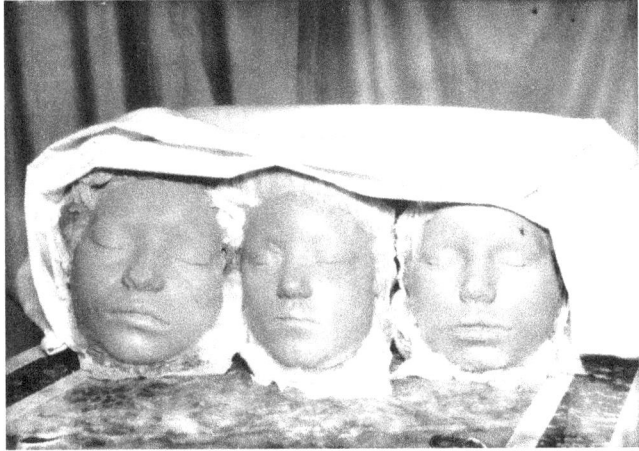

These death masks of the three sisters are currently in the CCHS museum collection.

We thank Thee for the woodsmen bold.
Who of their finding the wide world told;
We loved our lives—we sisters three,
But now we're thankful for the life to be.

It was reported how the Legion raised about $270 toward funeral expenses, the equivalent of about $4,281 in 2009. Donations came from businesses, organizations and individuals from cities as far away as Hanover and Philadelphia. The Legion received many offers from people out of state willing to assist in burying the girls. One offer was from Willard Rockefeller of New York, whose telegraph read: "I will gladly furnish graves for the three unfortunate kiddies in my family plot to save them from a pauper's burial."

Rockefeller had one condition: the Legion had to ship the bodies to the Albany, New York railroad station, where they would be picked up. Binkley declined but expressed his appreciation for the offer in a return letter to Rockefeller. As local residents came together to give the sisters a dignified burial, the state police assigned more than one hundred investigators to solve the mystery. In the end, they interviewed about three thousand people nationwide within a week and pursued clues as far away as California, where the story actually began two weeks before the bodies were found.

A preliminary autopsy conducted on November 24 revealed no apparent cause of death, so the girls were X-rayed at Carlisle Hospital and brought back to the funeral home shortly before midnight. A Harrisburg pathologist would later examine the sisters and conclude that they died from either strangulation or suffocation. George Moffitt based his conclusions on congested areas in the victims' brains and on signs of nasal hemorrhaging found on the youngest and oldest sisters. The murder weapon could have been a soft cloth, a pillow or blanket. These examinations also found that the victims had consumed no food during the eighteen hours prior to death and had been placed on the mountain sometime between 8:30 p.m. and midnight on November 23 but before the onset of rigor mortis. They had been dead between twelve and seventy-two hours before they were found.

Speculation ran wild on what happened to the children. Dr. Wilbur Norcross, head of the psychology department at Dickinson College, advanced the theory that the parents may have killed the girls as a religious sacrifice. He suggested that police check out places where revivals are being held or were held recently.

Experienced in criminal cases, Norcross based his theory on a mark resembling the Latin cross on the forehead of the middle sister. He believed that the girl may have been singled out for sacrifice before the parents killed the other sisters to spare them the grief. The parents may have attached special significance to a Bible verse or "labored under the obsession their children would be better off in Heaven," Norcross said. This theory was supported by how the girls were tucked away in death.

The same day the girls were found, Elmo Noakes, thirty-two, and Winifred Pierce, eighteen, his niece and lover, were found dead outside Altoona in an apparent murder-suicide. The evidence would eventually link the deaths together and identify the children as twelve-year-old Norma Sedgwick and her two half sisters, eight-year-old Cordelia and ten-year-old Dewilla Noakes. One theory, which proved true, was that Elmo Noakes was related to the sisters and had killed them because he was broke and wanted to spare them from poverty. He was identified as Norma's stepfather and the father of Cordelia and Dewilla. But the motive goes deeper.

As the story goes, Elmo's wife died in 1932, leaving him alone to raise the sisters in Roseville, California. Six months before the tragedy, Pierce had quit high school and had become his housekeeper. While she stayed at home and cared for the children, he worked at the Pacific Fruit Express Company.

Friends and relatives sensed a growing romance between Noakes and Pierce, but blood kinship proved to be a barrier to their love. This caused so much conflict that the families stopped talking to each other. On November 11, 1934, Elmo Noakes made the hasty decision to leave behind California and the bitter family objections that hindered a relationship with Pierce.

There is speculation that the former marine was emotionally overwrought or feared revenge from Pierce's male relatives. Elmo Noakes left California without collecting two weeks back pay, and there was evidence of a sudden flight at the family cottage. Part of a meal was still on the kitchen table, and the children's dolls were on their beds.

The couple drove across country, taking less than a week to travel about three thousand miles, and were seen in a restaurant in north Philadelphia on November 18. A witness told police that she noticed how tired and hungry the children looked. She even offered to buy the youngest child dinner.

During the meal, Cordelia Noakes told the woman that her family had just driven from California and that her father was trying to find work. "We've been going all the time," the girl said. "I'm kind of tired."

Investigators traced the family to a tourist camp in Langhorne north of Philadelphia. Camp operators told police that the couple traveled in a 1929 Pontiac sedan under the alias of Mr. and Mrs. J.C. Malone of Vallejo, California. The family stayed at the camp from Monday, November 19 to Wednesday, November 21, when they left. Police believe that this was the day the three children were murdered.

Police were able to connect the family to a suitcase that a hunter found on November 22 about two and a half miles from where the sisters were found. Among the items in the suitcase was a souvenir puzzle book given out by Standard Oil Company with the name "Norma" written in childlike script on the front cover. Investigators learned that no such booklets were distributed in the Northeast, leading them to believe the children were from another part of the country.

Also important to solving the case was a 1929 Pontiac sedan found abandoned in a field midway between Grove Mills and McVeystown about forty miles east of Altoona. While it had no license plate, a check of its identification number revealed that the car had been sold to Elmo Noakes on November 10.

Investigators believed that on November 22 the couple spent the night at a boardinghouse in Altoona. The next day, Pierce sold her coat—their last remaining possession other than the clothes they were wearing. Noakes then used the money to buy a rusty .22-caliber rifle from a secondhand shop. He then killed Pierce with bullets through the heart and brain before turning the gun on himself.

Police believed that the motive was one of desperation. Unable to land a job, Noakes was destitute and could not provide for his family, nor did he wish to return to the squabbling he left behind in California. Throughout their journey, the couple took pains to conceal themselves from relatives. This may be why they removed the license plate from the car and destroyed all identifying paperwork.

The caskets of the three sisters as they are being carried out of Ewing Funeral Home.

The night before the funeral, a viewing was held during which one thousand people filed past the open caskets to catch one final glimpse of the sisters dressed alike in soft white garments. The next morning, a short private service was held at the funeral home with guests that included a Legion honor guard, along with local boy scouts and girl scouts, who served as pallbearers. A *Sentinel* reporter, watching from the hallway, described the scene: "Baskets and sheaves of flowers circled the caskets…The white caskets each identical to the other bore silver plates inscribed with the words 'At Rest.'"

Five hundred people waited outside the funeral home for the procession to Westminster Cemetery in North Middleton Township. Under stormy skies, three snow-white caskets were lowered in the same relative positions as how the bodies were found under the blanket. Cordelia, the youngest, was in the middle, with Norma, the oldest, to her right and Dewilla to the left. The *Sentinel* reported how Mother Nature seemed to mourn this tragic loss of innocence: "Rain churned by a strong north wind beat a solemn staccato on upturned umbrellas and nearly drowned out the commitment prayers offered by the three officiating clergymen."

Post members later stood guard over the girls' burial plot to prevent souvenir seekers from mutilating the sod and flowers around the grave. The *Sentinel* published an editorial in its November 30 edition that recapped the solution of the mystery as a lesson on how mental illness or overwrought emotion could lead to tragedy. The writer concluded: "The reaction will be one of pity rather than blame…The mind is a most delicate organ, and despite the best conditions physical, economic and mental, it sometimes breaks down."

PART III
GALLOWS GROUND

Hangings in Carlisle were often scenes of public spectacle. Thousands of area residents would gather to witness the final moments of the condemned pass by as defiant protests of their innocence. What was known as Gallows Ground occupied a spot near what locals now call the "Point," where Trindle and York Roads intersect with East High Street. Executions were later moved about two blocks to the west to the rear yard of the old county jail. No matter what the crime or venue, the end result was always a quick snap, followed by justice dangling at the end of a rope.

A Most Dastardly Pursuit: The Murder of David Musselman

Those who found David Musselman, lying under the tree, had seen dead bodies mutilated by the Indians. But none were so dreadfully mangled as this unfortunate traveler discovered on the road to Carlisle. His gun was found by him, broken up in pieces, along with a bludgeon steeped in blood with its end shivered off to resemble a hickory broom. It was Monday morning, January 8, 1787.

It was plainly obvious, from the blood and tracks in the snow, that there had been a desperate struggle the night before. Witness John Junken said that the impact of strokes off in the distance sounded like the cutting of saplings. He had also heard a gun or pistol being discharged. But Junken thought it was only teamsters setting up camp and kindling a fire, so he did not investigate.

Old-timers living along the road would pass down stories of how they heard the hoofs of galloping horses rattled over the stone and cries of David Musselman echo through the night. Witness testimony established that Joseph Ramsay Warner had ordered Musselman to stop and hand over his money, but the victim spurred on his horse and thus sealed his fate.

The pursuit was on, up and down hills for a distance of twelve miles, before Warner caught up with Musselman just below present-day New Kingston and knocked the victim from his horse with a club. After that, the gory details are sketchy on this highway robbery turned murder, but there was no denying justice for poor Musselman. Before it was over, Warner would face the hangman's noose on Gallows Ground just outside Carlisle.

A man arrived at Harris Ferry the morning of Sunday, January 7, 1787. He told witnesses that he had traveled a great distance just to meet up with a friend at this crossing over the Susquehanna River. The man had waited a

The Harris Ferry House, built circa 1734, is in the foreground, with the Susquehanna River in the background. This house was once owned by William Kelso, original owner of the slave Chloe, whose story appears earlier in the book.

long time before David Musselman showed up on his way to Bedford County after first visiting relatives in Lancaster County, where he used to live.

Witnesses testified that the men crossed the river together, but it did not appear to them that Musselman knew his traveling companion nor did they seem to take notice of each other. The stranger only grumbled about the price of the ferry and mentioned how he was almost out of money.

The two men were seen riding together to John Walker's tavern, where Musselman stopped for dinner and to have his horse fed. The stranger also fed his horse. As they departed, the victim looked at his watch and said it was 7:02 p.m. That was the last time he was seen alive. It was later learned that Warner, a Chester County resident, had heard that Musselman was carrying a large sum of money and thus planned to lay in wait for him at the ferry crossing located in present-day Harrisburg.

It turned out that Warner was foiled by his own horse, which ran away while the two men were engaged in the life-or-death struggle around the tree. Warner had to use the victim's horse for his getaway after he first robbed the corpse of the money and the watch. It would appear that Warner's horse returned to the crime scene, because witnesses testified that they found the animal near the body but could not find the horse Musselman had used the night he was murdered.

The *Carlisle Gazette*, in its January 10 edition, reported on the public reaction to the grisly discovery: "The community was immediately alarmed all around. The people deserve praise for their spirited endeavors to apprehend the murderer."

The newspaper explained how a man unaware of the murder came upon a saddled horse standing in the road that matched the description of the animal the victim was seen riding. This witness led the horse to Lisburn, where he saw a man crossing Yellow Breeches Creek in a canoe. He thought the horse belonged to the man in the canoe. But when the ferryman returned, he mentioned how the clothes of his passenger were bloody. The bystanders then suspected foul play and immediately raised the alarm throughout the countryside. They were soon joined by others, who confirmed that a traveler had been murdered.

Within two minutes, they saw a man meeting the description of the person who had crossed the creek in the canoe. They seized him and accused him of murder. The man, later identified as Warner, denied the charges and then tried to escape. He even drew a pistol when he was pursued. Warner was immediately recaptured and searched.

Citizens found on him even more incriminating evidence, including two pocket pistols, fifty-six dollars and a watch in his jacket pocket. The newspaper reported Warner's reaction to being searched: "When the money was taken out of his pocket, there were some small money in a pocket by itself, when that was laid hold of, he said, 'that is my own,' and on being asked to whom the rest belonged, said it was his own also."

Perhaps the most damaging evidence were the articles of clothing that relatives in Lancaster identified as the ones they made for Musselman's children. The newspaper reported how Warner, when confronted with the obvious, admitted to crossing the river the same time as the victim and being with the deceased at the tavern. However, he claimed that they were jumped by two men, who knocked him down and assaulted the victim. Warner said that he made off, only to walk the whole night. He did not stop, even though he saw homes along the way. Warner said that he wanted to go to York as quickly as possible to advertise the disappearance of his horse.

The January 10 edition of the *Carlisle Gazette* had this to say about his guilt or innocence: "Whether he is the person who committed this crime, an impartial jury of this county will decide; far be it from us to prepossess the public against any person in the situation of the prisoner, and therefore we only state facts without attempting to draw any conclusion from them."

Four months later, on May 16, 1787, the *Carlisle Gazette* reported how the trial of Joseph Ramsay Warner "lasted upwards of five hours" but that the

The Walker Tavern once stood at the intersection of Route 11 and Rich Valley Road and operated during the Revolutionary War. It was demolished circa 1971.

jury delivered a guilty verdict in just three minutes without even leaving the box to deliberate on the case.

That June, Warner was escorted from the county jail at North Bedford and East High Streets to Gallows Ground by a contingent of light horse and infantry. There had gathered, as the newspaper reported, "the largest assemblage of people that had ever appeared on a like occasion in this county."

Even at the end, Warner denied his involvement in the murder.

"Hell's Fire Fury": The Execution of Ed Donnelly

It took some effort for Edward Donnelly to pry open the cold, stiff fingers of his wife, Catharine, only to close her grip on the handle of the shoemaker's knife. He then took her hand in his "endeavoring to make her cut my throat," but before the blade could slice open his flesh, Donnelly recalled her final words from the day before: "O Ned, if you kill me, take care of the children."

On the eve of his execution, Donnelly would confess the remorse he felt at that moment. "O what a horrid situation I was then in. I would have given the whole world if my wife was alive." But he would soon join her in death, and who can say to what fate Ed Donnelly condemned his soul—he killed not only his wife but also their unborn child and made orphans out of three other children. He then burned her body to ash in what he called a "Hell's fire fury."

When Donnelly died, a newspaper reporter was there to record his last three words spoken as the cap was drawn over his face and the noose was put around his neck: "I am gone." The *Carlisle Gazette* saw this as a lucid moment amid pretended insanity: "This did not look like want of reason, but sober reflection."

His hanging on February 8, 1808, was a public spectacle before an audience of three to four thousand people. A troop of cavalry and a company of infantry escorted the prisoner to the gallows. On the way, Donnelly made violent threats against those he deemed responsible for his arrest and conviction. He spat at people who drew too close. The newspaper went on to note, "He pretended sometimes he was God almighty, and that they could not hurt him. He was heard to say 'O God, destroy us all.'"

His death brought an end to public hangings in Cumberland County. The Pennsylvania General Assembly in 1834 required that future executions be carried out within the walls or yard of the county jail. Attendance would be restricted, and no one underage would be allowed to view a hanging.

This ad for a booklet on the case appeared in the *Cumberland Register* in February 1808.

The execution of Ed Donnelly even inspired a poem published along with his confession in the February 12, 1808 edition of the *Carlisle Gazette*. Following is an excerpt:

> *Ere twilight arrived on the eve of the day*
> *Which doom'd poor Ned Donnelly's corpse to the clay*
> *A band of dull loggerheads drag'd up the body*
> *And bawl'd it away, without cart, chair or noddy,*
> *But being detected, they scamper'd away*
> *And Neddy, once more was consign'd to the clay.*

Almost a century later, in 1901, former newspaperman George Shrom recalled a story his father told him on more than one occasion: "My father was a very small boy when this execution took place. He saw Ned swung off. Ned sat on his coffin on a cart and the entire distance from the jail he cried out, 'I was born to be hanged. I was born to be hanged.'"

Donnelly exhibited a pattern of erratic behavior. In his confession, he had said that he was born in Ireland in 1775 and lived there until age eighteen. He began his "career of wickedness" at age fifteen, "guilty of improper conduct with a female at my father's house." He did not elaborate on what that meant exactly, only to say that he left Ireland three years later arriving in the United States in 1794.

Donnelly settled in East Pennsboro Township, Cumberland County, and married Catharine Banden. The couple had three children, and his wife "was in a high state of pregnancy with the fourth" when Donnelly murdered her on August 9, 1807. He blamed his abusive behavior on alcoholism, saying that since arriving in North America he had "often been a subject to the sin of intoxication."

Donnelly confessed to an episode the day before the murder. He, his wife and eldest son of seven years old were out in the oat field harvesting grain when Donnelly asked his wife to go to the house and prepare dinner. He also asked his son to bring out a bottle of whiskey and some water. When his son returned with just water in a coffeepot, it made Donnelly angry, and he "swore a great oath" threatening to abuse his wife for not sending the whiskey bottle with the boy. He described what happened next: "She came round a different way from me with the bottle, which aggravated me more because I had to go back where she was with the bottle and whiskey…I then took a dram of whiskey and some water. I then fell to abuse my wife and struck her several times across the small of the back."

Donnelly said that a "woman of color" witnessed this beating and told him that "it was true what the people said, that I was a drunken rascal." He told her that she was the devil and threatened to cut off her head with a scythe. The violence only escalated from there: "When I had taken off the scythe off the cradle, the little boy [his son] began to run from me. I told him to stop but he did not. I then struck him with the scythe and cut him in the head and told him I would make him stop. My wife then took hold of the boy and threw him over the fence from me."

Drunk, Donnelly chased the colored woman, but she escaped. He then returned home; as Donnelly opened the door, his second son ran out and refused to stop when ordered. Donnelly struck this child with the scythe, also cutting the head. He felt remorse: "I then took him in my arms and carried him into the house and washed his head with cold water and laid him in the bed…finding him bleeding from the wound freely, frightened me so that I cried bitterly and thought I would take my own life."

Instead, Donnelly looked around the house and found a solution. He took some cobwebs and applied them directly to the wound, which stopped the bleeding immediately. Thinking himself clever, Donnelly drank more whiskey until he passed out, only to wake up the next morning.

He went outside and saw his wife and eldest son coming across the field. Donnelly got angry when they told him that they spent the night out in rye shock, which is a pile of grain. He had had nothing to eat since Saturday morning, so he ordered his wife to go to the house and prepare something to eat. He then went out into the field to retrieve items he left there from the day before. That is when Donnelly saw tracks as if someone had ridden through the oat field. He returned to the house "in a great passion."

Donnelly was jealous of his wife, convinced that she was cheating on him, although he had no proof of infidelity. He demanded to know the identity of whoever made the tracks. When she denied any knowledge of anyone riding through the oats, he began to physically abuse her. She persisted in her denial, and Donnelly drank more liquor to work himself into a rage. He took up his gun and struck her with it, threatening to kill her if she did not divulge the identity of the mystery rider. "I then took the fire tongs and beat her severely. She still begging of me for God's sake not to kill her. I then quit beating her in the house, got the wagon whip and took my wife to the rye field to show me where the shock was and where she and the boy lay all night."

From this vantage point, Donnelly could see the horse tracks in the oat field. He only got angrier, using the whip to beat his wife until the lash flew off. She was screaming the whole time, but he paid no attention to her pleas. He then dragged her around the field, hitting her with the butt end of the whip and swearing that he would kill her. Then just before Donnelly struck the fatal blow, she asked him to take care of the children. After finding her dead, he picked her up in his arms and carried her to the rye shock, where he held her close in his arms all night. The children were left in the house all night by themselves.

The next morning, Donnelly carried his dead wife to the house, woke up his children and made them kiss their dead mother. He tried to convince them that she was asleep, but they knew otherwise. The youngest one, according to Donnelly, acted like a fool, expecting that prayer could bring his mother back to life. A short time later, Donnelly contemplated suicide while holding a knife to his throat in his wife's dead hand. But the outrage did not end there. Donnelly locked the two older children in the barn and then returned to the house with the youngest child. There he stoked a large fire in the hearth. His confession reads: "I then took her out of the bed and dashed her into the fire, at the same time swearing I would burn the Devil and send her into the elements with Hell's fire fury. I threw a quantity of wood into the fire on her, which made a fire so large that I, at that time, called it Hell's fury. [I] kept [on] turning her about until the flesh was burnt off her bones."

He checked on his children before returning to the house. In tending the fire, he saw that her head was still very much intact. He took it from the hearth and pounded up the bones with an axe before casting the fragments back into the fire. He forgot his children in the barn until next morning. He found them there eating green peaches. When he asked where they slept, they replied the hayloft. When he asked how they climbed to the loft, one of the boys said that "mommy was with them and lifted them up." When Donnelly took his children back to the house, they asked for their mother. He lied, telling them she had climbed out a window and ran away. As before, he locked his children up in the barn while he continued to dispose of the evidence. "I returned to the house and set to the residue of the bones. After I was done smashing the bones I carried out the greater part of the ashes and threw them on the ground. I remained in the place in a melancholy state, sometimes working and at other times drinking until the 17th day of August when I was taken and brought to prison."

Donnelly did not mention his children again in his written confession. Neighbors heard his wife scream and the sounds of the beating. They alerted the authorities, who investigated and found parts of her skull, teeth and lower jaw among the ashes from the hearth. No one believed his claims that she had run off and left him behind. Catharine Donnelly was not the type to abandon her children.

His trial the following November took two days, but the jury convicted Donnelly of murder after only thirty minutes of deliberation. A minor technicality delayed sentencing until January, when President Judge James Hamilton condemned Donnelly to the gallows with the following words critical of his attempt to hide the murder from justice:

> *Edward Donnelly, you have been convicted of an offence the most heinous in the sight of God and man, accompanied with circumstances of unexampled atrocity, enormity and barbarity…*

Without provocation, you thus cut off in the prime of life, this most unfortunate woman, at a period when her children, springing up around her, promised some solace to her afflictions after a series of years of… preserving cruelty…You vainly imagined your enormous guilt was hid from the eye of man…

An all seeing Providence which disappoints the designs of the wicked, had already prepared the means of its defeat—the assembled neighbors, with others, influenced by the worthiest motives, were conducted to the heap of ashes at the black oak, and from these…the sad remains of your murdered wife.

In pronouncing sentence, Judge Hamilton was convinced that alcoholism "debased, hardened and depraved" the mind of Edward Donnelly. He thought it was proper to hold up the condemned husband as a beacon for others to steer away from a course of vice and drunkenness "that they may avoid the rock upon which all your earthly prospects have been irrecoverably wrecked."

Hamilton recommended Donnelly seek out the counsel of local clergymen so he may find salvation in his final days. As before, Donnelly expressed some remorse.

"I often had a mind to kill myself while confined in prison," he said in his confession. "The night after I received the sentence of death by the court I made three attempts to take my life. One way, in particular, I had three sewing needles, broke off the points and swallowed them, expecting they would destroy me. I thought my wife appeared to me with the child on her lap."

The *Carlisle Gazette*, in its February 5, 1808 edition, reported how attempts were made "by divines and other pious persons" to win from Donnelly a confession of his crimes, but his behavior had been bizarre. "At times he would weep bitterly and, in a few minutes, appear again cheerful conversing on ordinary affairs."

The newspaper was convinced that this odd behavior was contrived insanity, and it seemed Edward Donnelly was unwilling to repent. That changed the night before his hanging, when he had this to say: "Often in my drunkenness, my wife told me to quit drinking. If I did not quit drinking, I would certainly do some mischief. She told me to swear against it…I told her if I did I would die."

Author's note: While many sources spell the murderer in this case as Edward "Donally," I went with the spelling in his published confession.

"A LIFE FOR A LIFE": THE PEOPLE V. CHARLES SALYARDS

There was nothing anyone could do to save police officer George Martin. The bullet had entered his chest at the third rib near the heart and cut a horizontal course through his right lung. Blood flowed from his nose and mouth and ran down the front of his shirt. He was dying within yards of the Old Graveyard.

Hal Martin was among the first to reach the body. He gently lifted his brother's head before letting it fall back again. He noticed how George tried to speak, but his tongue seemed paralyzed. The eyes gazed about before closing shut forever. So many hopes died that night with George Martin, a Carlisle native who was waiting for authorities to hire a replacement so he could resign and spend more time with his family.

The *Evening Sentinel* described Martin as a kindhearted man who never shirked his duty. The press said that proof of his fearlessness could be seen in how this officer, armed only with a club, chased a man with a revolver down a dark lane the evening of April 8, 1893. The newspaper called it a "most startling tragedy" and "a dastardly deed" that demanded justice no matter the cost.

Carlisle and Cumberland County posted rewards of $500 each for information leading to the arrest and conviction of the killer. Feeling her pain, the community rallied behind the widow and her child, with the *Sentinel* encouraging readers to donate money to a charity fund as the highest tribute paid to the memory of Martin.

Suspicion fell almost immediately on Charles Salyards, a known felon suspected in several robberies in downtown Carlisle. Days before the shooting, Carlisle police received a telegram from Chambersburg urging them to be alert for a middle-aged man with a long beard and glasses and dressed in dark clothes. It was widely believed, at the time of his death, that George Martin was shadowing Salyards.

Witnesses to the shooting saw a man fitting the description jump over a wall and run from the crime scene. The night of the murder, a local minister encountered a stranger on the road just outside Mount Holly Springs who claimed that his partner had been shot in Carlisle but that he did not know how seriously. Dispatches were sent by telegram in all directions, along with riders sent out to search for the suspect.

Investigators soon traced Salyards to Hagerstown, Maryland, where he bought new clothes and had his long beard trimmed short. He had registered at a hotel under an assumed name. From Hagerstown, the

This sketch of Charles Salyards appeared in the *Carlisle Weekly Herald* on March 1, 1894.

suspect boarded a train bound for Winchester, West Virginia, but was recognized by the brakeman, who tipped off the authorities. Salyards was arrested in Winchester and transported back to Carlisle, arriving four days after the shooting.

Word had spread rapidly of his imminent arrival. By the time the train arrived on April 12, hundreds of Carlisle residents had gathered around the station at the northwest corner of High and Pitt Streets waiting to exact vigilante justice. Authorities tried to fool the mob by stopping the train directly in front of the county jail about two blocks to the east. The crowd got wise to the ruse and hurried for the jail, but Salyards was safe inside a cell before they could organize. The *Sentinel* described the scene:

> *The space before the jail was packed with a solid mass of humanity…Several climbed the trees…to get a view of the prisoner. Officers appeared with their man and rushed him from the platform right through the crowd and the jail door closed behind them. The crowd howled and cries of "Shoot him…Kill him" were heard. Plenty of persons were ready to take the law into their hands but they lacked leaders…There were reports the jail would be stormed but better counsels prevailed.*

There was speculation that Salyards would have been lynched if he had to walk the two blocks between the train station and the jail. The reporter described the suspect as "pale and haggard," and though nervous, he seemed satisfied to be safe inside prison walls. But there was no escape from relatives of George Martin, who confronted the alleged murderer. It was said that Andrew Martin, the victim's cousin, glared at Salyards, clenched his fists and then turned away.

The *Carlisle Herald* reported that, when calm, the suspect presented a "genteel and intellectual appearance" but when angry, "a sinister form would come over his face and he looked devilish." A nervous man, Salyards was irritable and easily ruffled. The press described him as a coward who did not stay for long at any one place and only fought when he had the upper hand.

The *Sentinel*, in its April 13 edition, published Salyards's record, calling it "unsavory and criminal from beginning to end." He was known throughout the valley having committed crimes in Carlisle, Mount Holly Springs, Harrisburg and Chambersburg over the past twenty years. He had spent one third of his life behind bars on prior charges including a couple stints in state prison.

In a prior case, Salyards acted as his own attorney but ended up serving time. He was without a lawyer when he was brought before court for formal arraignment in May. Defense attorneys were recruited on the spot and demanded a continuance after the prosecutor pressed to have the trial start in two days. The court ruled in favor of the Commonwealth after the district attorney announced that Salyards had already had weeks to prepare his case. Up to that point, Salyards refused to have the court appoint him an attorney.

The defense team also requested a change of venue given the public hostility and "inflammatory" press reports. In asking the judge to step down, the defense argued that the court had already showed its sympathy by attending Martin's funeral and donating money to the widow fund after their client was charged. The judge ruled against these pretrial motions.

During the trial, the prosecution tried to prove that Martin was pursuing Salyards the night of the shooting and that the defendant had lured Martin down a dark lane that passes along the east wall of the Old Graveyard—what is today South Bedford Street in Carlisle. The theory is that Salyards wanted to make good on his threats and draw the police officer out of town and away from witnesses.

This plan was allegedly foiled when Salyards came within one hundred yards of young men having a beer party partway down the lane. This forced Salyards to turn and fire on Martin before jumping over a nearby fence and escaping into the night.

To back this claim, the district attorney called Mr. and Mrs. John Filor to the stand. They testified that Salyards had recently stayed overnight at their house on Dickinson Alley. When they noticed that Salyards had a revolver, they asked him about it. The defendant replied that if the police continued to follow him, he would give them something they didn't want.

A fellow houseguest gave even more damaging testimony. Edward Lytle told jurors that Salyards said if that "squinty-eyed son of a bitch Martin doesn't leave me alone, I'll give him lots of cold lead." Lytle, who was blind, then felt something against the tip of his nose. Reaching up, he felt the barrel of a revolver pointed at his head and heard Salyards say, "I could put a bullet through you."

On the stand, Salyards disputed this testimony and said that he made no threats against Martin. He claimed that the couple was too drunk to even notice a revolver. His attorneys argued that the statements of Lytle and the Filors were so different for the same alleged event they could scarcely be believed.

Several prosecution witnesses testified to seeing Martin chase Salyards minutes before both men entered Graveyard Lane. Mrs. James Hollinger lived on the corner of Bedford and South Streets. She identified the defendant in court as the man being pursued by Martin.

Elizabeth Dinkledine testified to seeing both men pass her home on Chapel Alley before emerging onto Bedford Street. She later changed her testimony to where she could not positively identify Salyards as the man followed by Martin. On the stand, Salyards denied seeing Dinkledine that night and claimed that her testimony was motivated by spite over his involvement with her daughter. It was brought out during the appeal that Dinkledine knew the defendant and that her seventeen-year-old daughter had frequently visited Salyards while he was in jail. Four years prior, Salyards wanted the girl to elope with him.

Testifying in his own defense, Salyards denied any knowledge of the shooting or of being chased by Martin that night. The murder took place on the south side of Carlisle at about 9:45 p.m. The defendant claimed that at that time he was visiting friends on the north side of town about a half-mile away from the crime scene. He left their home at about 10:10 p.m. The friends corroborated this alibi. Salyards then walked to the train station on West High Street, where he stowed away on a train bound for Hagerstown. Salyards said that at no point did he venture into the south side of town that night.

In their opening statement, defense attorneys portrayed Martin as an officer with a bad temper who was prone to violently assaulting people on more than one occasion. They claimed that the lack of preparation time caused by the denial of the continuance hindered them from fully developing this part of their case. It was reported how they had trouble on such short notice trying to find witnesses willing to testify to Martin's past behavior. Even if Salyards was running that night, the defense claims that it was not to lure Martin down a dark lane but rather to evade a hotheaded cop.

Defense attorneys also argued that just because their client may have threatened police doesn't mean he was going to carry out the threats. They called to question forensic evidence of shoe prints found in a field that investigators believed belong to the shooter fleeing the crime scene. The prosecution argued that the shoe size matched that of Salyards, but the defense countered that running on soft ground causes a larger print, so the actual shoe size had to be smaller.

The defense also questioned whether the men at the beer party were sober enough to accurately recall seeing the shooter flee the scene. There was even speculation by the defense that one of the men at the party may have shot Martin. The jury only had the word of the men that there was no revolver among them. In the end, the jurors only took three hours to convict Salyards of murder.

In their subsequent appeal, the members of the defense team moved for a new trial, arguing that a change of venue should have been ordered given the hostility of the public and inflammatory press reports. In response, the judge said that the coverage was no different in tone to what was reported in prior murder cases.

The defense also alleged jury misconduct, saying that Levi Goodyear of Monroe Township testified during voir dire that he had not formed an opinion on the case when indeed he had. He even bet a friend five dollars that he would get on the jury based on his answers. Defense attorneys also called the case a "persecution," not a prosecution, of Salyards, claiming that investigators only focused on building a case against their client and not following other trails of evidence or possible theories on who could have killed Martin.

In requesting a new trial, the defense also alleged that jurors were impaired in their ability to properly deliberate on the case by a court order treating them to three shots of whiskey daily. The *Sentinel* reported it as follows: "Those jurors, farmers as they were and not accustomed to weighing evidence, needed a full head on them when passing upon a case of life and death and for them to have even one drink under the circumstances was nothing short of cruel."

The court, in denying the motion for a new trial, said it was presumed that the jurors were accustomed to drinking that much alcohol per day.

⊹THIS WILL ADMIT⊹

Harry Harnish

To the execution of Charles Salyards on
~~MAR 1 1894~~
January 23, 1894, at 10:30 A. M.

⊰NOT TRANSFERABLE.⊱

Geo B Struck, Sheriff.

Sheriff's Office, Carlisle, Pa.

This ticket to Salyards's execution is now in the CCHS archives.

The judge added that there was no evidence to suggest that jurors were intoxicated during any of the court proceedings and that alcohol was only furnished to them during the meal breaks. At the time, there was no law forbidding alcohol use by jurors in a capital case.

This issue came up again when the defense filed an appeal before the Pennsylvania Pardons Board to have the death sentence against Salyards commuted to life in prison. A.F. Mullin, a paper manufacturer from Mount Holly Springs, wrote a letter dated January 3, 1894, in support of this appeal, which the *Sentinel* then published in its entirety two days later. In the letter, Mullin stated that he had never spoken to Salyards and had only seen the defendant in the courtroom. Thus, he had no personal interest in the matter but was writing about what he perceived was an injustice. Here is an excerpt:

> *It is the right of every man to have a fair trial by a jury of his peers. I am told...this man Salyards has been, all his life, strictly temperate, at least as far as the use of intoxicants is concerned, yet he was convicted by a jury, most...of whose number were given three drinks of liquor a day. Now, whatever may be the technical meaning of the word "peers" in law, if I were tried by such a jury, I should not consider that I had been tried by my peers.*

The letter goes on to describe the possible evils of alcohol in this case and what Mullin thought was an unfair rush to justice by Carlisle residents driven on by raw emotion:

> *All expert authorities agree that alcohol paralyzes the nerves of the brain and confuses the judgment and consequently renders the thinker incapable of discriminating between probability and slight presumption and properly weighing the delicate points of evidence, which tend to confirm the guilt or innocence of a prisoner, especially one who is being tried for life…*
>
> *Here lies the danger to society tenfold more than if one guilty man escapes…A man is killed, say a respected and popular officer; the excitement and indignation of the populace are aroused; someone is guilty and must be punished. To appease the wrath of the people a man is suspected, against whom some circumstantial evidence is procured…the man is arrested and tried by a jury whose brains are muddled by alcohol and…because the sentiment of the people demands a life for a life, he is convicted.*

The appeal before the Pardons Board ultimately failed. Salyards was put on suicide watch. The February 28, 1894 edition of the *Sentinel* reported how he tried to kill himself by swallowing match heads dissolved in vinegar. A search found that the condemned man also had in his possession glass fragments along with iron rust he had scraped from the bars of his cell.

His execution was set for the morning of March 1, 1894. Tickets were made available for the hanging held in the yard of county prison. The *Carlisle Herald* reported how a crowd of about one thousand had gathered outside the jail, along with the two hundred people admitted to the execution.

Based on the press accounts, a reporter may have been allowed into the cellblock prior to the hanging. The *Carlisle Herald* reported how Salyards sat on a couch in his cell calmly awaiting the arrival of the sheriff, who could be heard ascending the iron steps to the second-tier gallery.

The sheriff then stepped into the doorway of the cell, and Salyards's hands were manacled behind him. He was then escorted out a rear corridor and into the prison yard, where the gallows waited. Because he refused to die with his boots on, Salyards was in his stocking feet as the noose was tightened around his neck and the black hood was put over his face. Just before the trapdoor was pulled, Salyards uttered one word—"Innocent!"— in a muffled voice. His neck was broken instantly. The March 8 edition of the *Sentinel* published excerpts from his farewell letter:

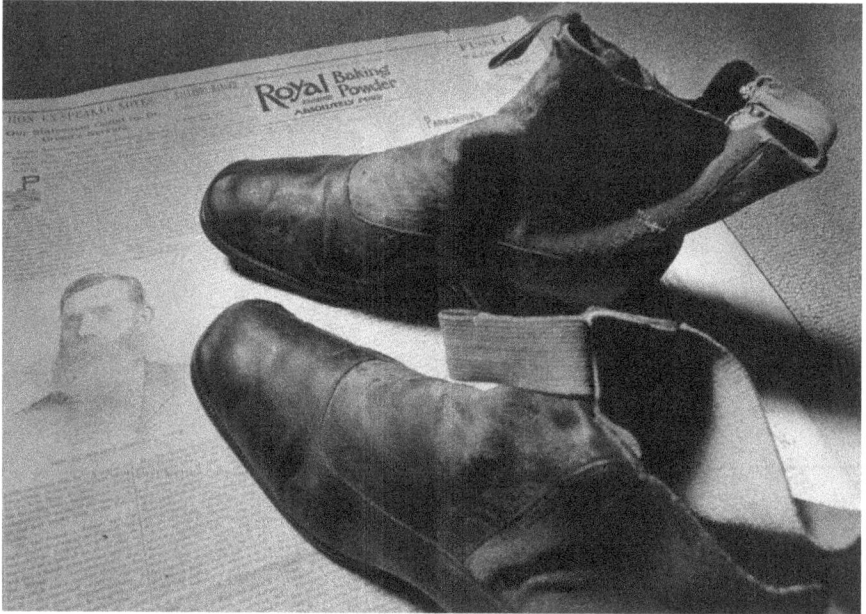

These are the boots that Salyards refused to wear on the day of his execution. They are now in the CCHS museum.

In taking leave of this beautiful world and all I hold dear, I want to say I never felt more like living than I do now, when…I have but a few hours to live. I do not fear to die, but I do fear the degradation of dying an undeserved death on the gallows. Yet I should prefer even that to the living death of a life sentence inside of the prison walls.

PART IV
HELL STREET BLUES

Local residents today enjoy good relations with the military stationed at Carlisle Barracks. A new class of students arrives each summer to attend the Army War College on post. They bring with them leadership ability, the spirit of community service and a welcome boost to the economy. It wasn't always this peaceful. Open hostility once existed between unsavory soldiers and townsfolk out to cause a ruckus. There was so much mayhem at one point that North Street from Bedford to East Streets became known as "Hell Street." As with any war, innocent bystanders—military and civilian—got hurt while caught in the crossfire.

"Peace to His Ashes": The McNamara Murder

They found John McNamara lying prone on the sidewalk, bleeding heavily and breathing his last. When Charles Jeremier heard the cry of "Murder!" he opened the bedroom window of his East Louther Street home and saw the body on the pavement. Another man, whom Jeremier took to be a soldier, was seen walking around the victim in a stooping posture, as if listening to hear if McNamara was dead. The man hovered for only a short time before leaving the scene. It was June 3, 1858, between midnight and 1:00 a.m. McNamara had been attacked only minutes before neighbors discovered his body.

Gathering around, they made the decision to carry the fallen soldier over to the vestibule of the old county courthouse on the Square, leaving him there until daybreak and a coroner's inquest. An autopsy determined that the thirty-three-year-old Irish immigrant died from massive bleeding after a dagger sliced an inch-and-a-half-deep cut into his chest, penetrating his heart. A soldier stationed at the post, he also suffered minor wounds to the left breast and abdomen. Those who knew McNamara described him as a peaceful, quiet and inoffensive man. Who could have killed him?

That same day, civilians felt deep sorrow as a funeral procession of about three hundred soldiers marched down Hanover Street to the Old Graveyard on East South Street. The post band played a solemn dirge as the hearse carrying the flag-draped coffin made its way slowly through town. The same carbine McNamara had used in a drill the day of his murder was strapped to his horse as it was lead to the grave site. In keeping with military tradition, McNamara's saddle boots were reversed in the stirrups. A reporter from the *American Volunteer* described the scene:

> *The big tear drop could be noticed in scores of eyes as the mangled body of the stranger was committed to the cold earth by fellow soldiers. Poor fellow—in the prime of his life, he was literally butchered in a public street of Carlisle with no one near him to whisper consolation in his dying hour. No one here*

The tombstone of John McNamara in the Old Graveyard in Carlisle. *Photo by Joseph Cress.*

has any knowledge of his lineage. He came to this country and joined our
Army, and fell by the coward hand of the assassin. Peace to his ashes.

While tension existed between the post and the Carlisle community, investigators suspected that another soldier, Francis Perrier, had murdered McNamara in what they believed was a case of mistaken identity. A cap belonging to Perrier was found ten to twelve feet from the body. That was just the first piece of circumstantial evidence against the thirty-five-year-old Frenchman described by one newspaper as a "hard looking customer" with downcast eyes and a swollen face.

News of the murder spread rapidly to the post, where an order was issued to arrest all men who had been in town the night before. Their clothing was examined, and when it was discovered that Perrier had lost a cap, he was brought into town for further questioning. Within his backpack, investigators found a pair of buckskin gloves that were slightly stained with blood. They also found a bloody dagger on East Street, not far from the crime scene.

Fellow soldiers testified that Perrier had had a fight in town with a soldier named Devlin two to three nights before the murder. Badly beaten about the face, Perrier had vowed revenge and purchased a six-inch dagger from one of the men. When first questioned by civilian authorities, Perrier said that he only owned a small pocketknife. He later admitted to owning a larger blade but claimed it had been lost the night of the murder along with his cap and some money.

Perrier testified that he was absent without leave the night of the murder drinking whiskey with friends. Perrier claimed that he had not seen the victim in Carlisle that evening and had only spoken to McNamara in passing before. They were not well acquainted. Perrier testified that he had no grudge against the victim nor had he ever made threats. He had left town and returned to post by about 11:00 p.m.

There were conflicting newspaper reports over whether Perrier had purchased the gloves the night of the murder or the night before. He testified that the blood was from an open sore on his hand and not from the victim. At trial, the defense argued that there was no positive proof that Perrier had committed the murder.

A jury that August found Perrier guilty of manslaughter, and he was sentenced to six years of solitary confinement in state prison. The verdict disappointed many local residents, but the *Carlisle Herald* explained that because the evidence was largely circumstantial, the jurors were duty-bound to find the defendant guilty of the lesser offense.

All along, prosecutors thought that Perrier had mistaken McNamara for Devlin in the darkness and had murdered the wrong man by accident. This theory would prove to be incorrect as evidenced by the defendant's own confession published in the *American Volunteer* after his conviction.

In it, Perrier said that he met Devlin in town the evening of the murder and even drank a few rounds with him. He was afraid to attack Devlin because his intended victim was suspicious and kept a close watch. Perrier and Devlin parted ways at about 11:30 p.m., leaving Perrier upset at himself as he walked back to post for not going through with his plan for revenge.

On his way, Perrier was allegedly overtaken by McNamara, who had also been in town drinking. They were soon joined by a couple other soldiers also heading back to the garrison. According to Perrier, they had just passed Bedford Street when a dispute arose between himself and McNamara, although Perrier did not elaborate on what caused the argument. Perrier claimed that McNamara struck him first and that he had only stabbed McNamara in self-defense. In his own words, Perrier "got to work on his assailant."

Perrier could not recall how many times he stabbed McNamara, only that the last cut was the fatal one. It was McNamara's cry of "Murder!" that summoned neighbors to the scene. Perrier lost his cap during the scuffle and immediately returned to his quarters.

Almost five years later, another soldier would be a victim of violence on the streets of northeast Carlisle. His killer would confess on the witness stand but leave the courtroom a free man.

"No Earthly Tribunal": The Gambler Who Wagered the Truth

Corporal John Barney was in charge of a detachment sent out the night of March 17, 1863, to find two soldiers who were absent without leave from evening roll call. Before the borough had an organized police force, soldiers on post routinely patrolled the streets nearest the barracks.

At 9:30 p.m., Barney and two soldiers were walking south on North East Street when they heard the sounds of a brawl up ahead in front of the McManus house, which still stands on the corner of Locust Avenue. They rushed to the scene only to find two women fighting as several men cheered them on. Barney demanded to know what was going on, but someone shouted that it was none of his business. He called out "Halt!" when some of the men tried to leave.

The McManus House.

While accounts vary, it is agreed Barney drew his sword and that one of the men fired a gun at the corporal. Barney was hit but pursued the culprit down the alley. More shots were fired, but the shooter managed to escape. Mortally wounded, Barney was carried back to the post, where he died about thirty-six hours later. The first bullet proved to be fatal, hitting its victim on the left side and piercing the liver.

One of the women, Kate Myers, identified James Marshall as the gunman, along with William Fields and Charlie Foulk as accomplices. The state charged all three with murder. After the prosecution rested its case, defense attorney William H. Miller asked the court to instruct the jury to find Foulk not guilty. Miller argued that none of the testimony directly linked his client to the shooting.

Judge James Graham agreed. The jury acquitted Foulk without even leaving the box, clearing the way for Miller to call the former defendant as a defense witness. But before Foulk would testify, he insisted on asking Graham one key question in a calm voice: "Can I ever be tried again for killing that soldier?"

It is believed that Graham knew what was coming next but still assured Foulk that the rule against double jeopardy applied in this case: "So far as human law is concerned, you are a free man. No earthly tribunal can try you again…only the great Judge before whom we must all be arraigned."

Foulk then announced that the jury had acquitted the wrong man, and to the surprise of most everyone in the courtroom, he described in great detail the murder he had committed. Foulk claimed that he only fired in self-defense after Barney drew his sword and attacked first, slashing Foulk's face and arm. Foulk said that he continued to fire as he was pursued down the alley by Barney, who continued to call "Halt!" before collapsing.

Meanwhile, Foulk escaped but fell into the Letort Spring. Soaked, he returned to the scene after everyone had left to retrieve his hat. His first shot was the only one that hit Barney. While Foulk claimed self-defense, historian D.W. Thompson wrote how there is evidence to suggest that the murder may have been premeditated to settle an old score. That night, Foulk returned home briefly from barhopping to retrieve two handguns before setting out again with friends. He was walking in an area known to be patrolled by soldiers.

Thompson described Foulk as a tall, handsome and refined gentleman known for running a gambling house in Carlisle. His friends thought of him as brave, while his enemies touted him as brave only when he has the advantage over someone. His confession that day in the courtroom raised enough reasonable doubt for the jury to acquit Marshall and Fields and for the public to make Foulk a popular hero.

Somehow Foulk managed to stay out of prison despite being charged over the years with murderous assault, arson and even bombing the house of Sheriff McCartney, an old rival. Along the way, Foulk married the chief constable's daughter and purchased the lot at 151 West Pomfret Street.

While waiting for trial on an arson charge, Foulk skipped bail and ended up in Hot Springs, Arkansas, where he won popular acclaim as a Mississippi River gambler until he himself was murdered. He was buried in the Old Graveyard on East South Street in Carlisle.

"THE ADVENT OF THIEVES": TENSIONS WITH THE MILITARY

Trouble was brewing long before the pair of army officers galloped their horses through downtown Carlisle. A rally was being held on the Square that Saturday, October 8, 1860, and the intersection of Hanover and High Streets was crowded with people. It was clear to borough police that the soldiers were breaking the law. The *Carlisle Herald* reported how the officers, upon realizing this, promptly offered to pay the fine, but some of the recruits in town decided to interfere with the local law enforcement. The newspaper reported what happened next: "Owing to the crowd, and excitement, some difficulty arose, and one of the soldiers who was mounted, while endeavoring to get his horse out of the crowd, which pressed on him from all sides, was struck by a stone and dragged to the ground."

Town constables arrested the soldier—not to commit him, but rather to spare him further injury—but this led to the rumor that he was being held in jail on charges. At about 6:30 p.m., a group of about forty soldiers marched from the garrison into town, each armed with a club or a stone. They stopped in front of the old county jail at High and Bedford Streets and demanded to see the civilian authority in charge of the building.

The *American Volunteer* reported how Sheriff McCartney appeared and asked the mob what they wanted. The tension level quickly jumped from uneasy talks to virtual riot, as documented in the newspaper coverage:

Several of them commenced to abuse the Sheriff, and threatened to storm the prison. By this time, a number of citizens had collected, and the Sheriff

The old Cumberland County Jail.

summoned them to assist him in dispersing the mob…The citizens rushed upon the soldiers, and for a time brick-bats and stones could be seen flying in all directions. The soldiers took to their heels, but several were dropped during their flight. The citizens followed them to Garrison Lane, and soon after the soldiers were safely on post.

The mob mistakenly believed that their comrade was still being held when there were no soldiers imprisoned. The *American Volunteer* published this strong warning to those at the post in its October 11, 1860 edition: "Should any of their number ever commit a breach of the peace, however, and be sent to prison, all the soldiers of the garrison will not be able to take him out, and we advise them not to make the attempt. We have no unkind feelings for the soldiers, but we tell them in all kindness that when they visit town they must behave themselves."

Vacant for some time, Carlisle Barracks was partially reestablished in early 1856 as a stopover for several hundred recruits passing through every year to receive training for the light artillery and cavalry service. The post was operated by a small staff. As a result, training was inadequate and discipline poor.

Come payday, groups of enlisted men went into town looking for a good time, only to get into fights with local ruffians. There were reports of soldiers spending off-duty hours or going absent without leave to annoy farmers and raid gardens and orchards of produce. At other times, organized bands came into Carlisle armed with sabers and carbines to break into private homes, discharge their weapons in the street and commit other crimes.

When ordinary measures failed, the army confined soldiers to the post to keep them from visiting the saloons, dance halls and brothels of Carlisle's east end. When civilian complaints to the commandant failed to offer relief, a citizen's committee organized a protest at the old courthouse to discuss how to bring grievances before the War Department. A poster signed by attorney William H. Miller announced the meeting. In it, he outlined the following propositions:

First. Either those outrages of the soldiers at our Garrison cannot be prevented, in which case this is not the proper place for a military school or garrison. It should be somewhere else than a thickly settled community, large numbers of whose citizens follow agricultural pursuits, and are constantly exposed to their outrages; or

William H. Miller.

Second. They can be prevented, in which case there has been woeful, culpable negligence somewhere and it behooves you, and every man who has the spirit of man in him, to enquire where the fault is, and have it redressed.

The strained relations only got worse, leading to frequent spells of violence along with a string of suspected arsons that destroyed several buildings at the post and almost persuaded the War Department to abandon Carlisle Barracks.

On January 5, 1857, the post bakery was destroyed by fire, followed seventeen days later by the officers' quarters, which cost the War Department an estimated $25,000 to rebuild. Then came a fire on May 18, 1857, that destroyed the large stables on the north side of the post. The stables had been rebuilt after an August 1851 blaze.

Early in 1860, the garrison staff was increased to more than two hundred cavalrymen to train recruits coming in from outlying stations in Baltimore, Philadelphia, Boston, New York City, Albany, Louisville and Cleveland.

These soldiers were stationed at Carlisle Barracks in the late 1800s.

Training was completed as quickly as possible so these men could be deployed westward to man frontier forts and serve as replacements for units fighting the Indians.

Disciplinary problems continued into the Civil War years and beyond, but the soldiers were not always at fault. The garrison tried to win the goodwill of town residents. Troops marched in the 1860 Fourth of July parade, while the post band often provided music for community events. During this period, civilians were guilty of their own outrages beyond the suspected arsons.

For example, local farmers would often visit the post to watch the soldiers drill and to sell them fresh fruit at exorbitantly high prices to reap huge profits. Captain Daniel Hastings, commandant during the war, suspected these abuses and had threatened to remove the profiteers from government land.

Perhaps the most glaring abuses by civilians came after the Confederate army retreated from its occupation of Carlisle on June 30, 1863, to fight the Union army at Gettysburg during the Southern invasion of Pennsylvania.

Deputy Sheriff Simpson K. Donavin reported how Confederate general Richard Ewell had intended to destroy the barracks but was talked out of it by local women who had been friends of his when he was stationed in Carlisle some years before. After Ewell left, a crowd of "lewd and depraved men and women" plundered the barracks, destroying furniture and stealing any clothing and blankets they could find.

"The Rebels had not destroyed any of the records of the post, but the prostitutes and their friends did not consider anything sacred," Donavin wrote. "Blank leaves in the ledgers were torn out, and the paper generally scattered in any direction. The place was made thrice more desolate by this advent of thieves."

The Confederate army would later return to Carlisle on July 1, 1863, when they shelled the town and burned the barracks. Already unpopular with the townspeople, Hastings was relieved of duty in April 1864 amid mounting pressure from civilians who accused him of favoritism and the misappropriations of funds in awarding contracts associated with the Carlisle Barracks reconstruction project.

There were lighter moments amid all the tension. While the post hospital was being rebuilt, women from town provided food and clothing to the sick and wounded. They also prepared a surprise Thanksgiving dinner at the new hospital in 1863 and 1864. But even gestures such as these could not stop the tension from taking an even more violent turn.

"SCENE OF TERROR AND CONFUSION": THE RIOT OF 1867

It can be said that Election Day is a day of reckoning. The old order bows to the new in a controlled upheaval of power that always seems to leave behind casualties. But on March 16, 1867, there came a day of chaos and pain brought on by lingering frustration between the soldiers of Carlisle Barracks and the civilians of Carlisle Borough. The resulting riot left two dead and about a dozen wounded, thus inflicting more casualties than the shelling of the town almost four years prior by the Army of Northern Virginia during the invasion of Pennsylvania.

Early that evening, local residents Augustus Hamill and John Gilmer got into a fight with two soldiers on the public square. It was reported that shots were fired during this incident—probably by Hamill, who was seen holding a pistol. The men bested the soldiers, who escaped to the post and, in swearing revenge, told their comrades what had happened.

The old Cumberland County Courthouse, decorated with patriotic bunting for a community event.

The *American Volunteer* reported how a group of 25 to 50 soldiers assembled at about 8:00 p.m. armed with carbines, sabers and revolvers. They marched west on East Louther Street to North Hanover Street and south to the Square, where they stopped on the railroad tracks facing the north side of the old courthouse. There a crowd of 150 to 200 local residents had gathered to wait for election returns. They had hit the polls earlier in the day.

The newspaper reported how the bitterness between the "roughs of the borough" and "some of the more lawless and disorderly…of soldiers" was made worse by recent fights in the saloons and dance halls of East Louther Street. An ugly scene greeted the soldiers, who were first subjected to jeers and insults, followed soon after by sticks and stones. The order was then given for the ranks to fire a volley into the crowd of unarmed civilians. The *American Volunteer* described what happened next:

> *Those who were able sought refuge in the Courthouse, and others fled in every direction. Stores and hotels immediately closed, and there was a universal shutting of windows and bolting of doors. It took but a minute or so for the citizens, thus taken by surprise, to rally in self-defense. The outrageous and unjustifiable firing into a crowd of unarmed men aroused the indignation of the whole community.*

In seconds, the whole Square was empty except for the soldiers who dominated the scene. Then civilians armed with handguns began to reach cover and return fire while others, including veterans, retrieved their weapons from storage and returned to the Square from all quarters of town to help fellow residents.

"For a few minutes, the bullets whistled thick and fast, and the riot had the appearance of a regular engagement," the newspaper reported. The civilians soon had the soldiers in full retreat down Church Alley and Hanover Street. The soldiers tried to rally and make a stand on East Louther Street but were beaten off. This time, they retreated to Carlisle Barracks, taking their wounded with them.

Several civilians were hurt, including Thomas Zimmerman, who was shot through the right forearm with a carbine ball. The bone was shattered, and it looked as though the arm would have to be amputated. The newspaper also reported how Jacob Schmohl was slightly wounded in the left hand. Neither of these men participated in the firefight but happened to be passing through the Square when the shooting began. The *American Volunteer* also mentioned how Mrs. Stuart was shot through the foot while standing at the door of her home on East Louther Street.

Sometime during the incident, General Grier, commandant of the post, dispatched a unit of the Sixth Cavalry under the command of Captain Kerns to arrest and return the wayward soldiers to the post. But the hyped-up civilians interpreted this action as the army sending reinforcements, so they opened fire. A sergeant named Bergman was shot through the head and killed by Gilmer. Other soldiers were wounded in this attack. Kerns withdrew his command back to the barracks. Order was only restored after Grier sent an entire troop of cavalry into the town.

After the riot, Hamill and another man had gone beyond Letort Bridge on East Louther Street when they were confronted by two soldiers, who

This illustration shows what may be the March 1867 street riot in Carlisle.

ordered them to halt and lay down their arms. Hamill refused to cooperate and was shot through the lungs by one of the soldiers. Hamill survived until about 10:00 p.m. His remains were buried in the Old Graveyard along East South Street. The funeral was attended by a large number of local residents, including members of the Cumberland Fire Company, of which Hamill was a member.

The *American Volunteer* described the riot as a "scene of terror and confusion" and a "dastardly attack upon unarmed civilians." The newspaper was ready to fix the blame on Grier for allowing armed bands of soldiers to come into town night after night "bent on their lawless errands." In its coverage of the riot, the *American Volunteer* mixed news and commentary in the same article:

> We are not informed whether the commandant…was aware of the depredations nightly committed by men under his charge, but he ought to have known of them, as they were matters of common report. There must be something vitally wrong in his system of government…Better discipline than this might be expected in a transient volunteer camp and ought to be at all times enforced in a permanent garrison of the regular army.

The newspaper was kinder with local officials, saying that the riot was so sudden and violent there was nothing the authorities could have done to quell it. "It is worse than folly to talk of a burgess and three constables suppressing such a disturbance and it was just as useless for the Sheriff to attempt to get an armed posse of staid and sober citizens to interfere amidst the flying bullets of fifty or sixty infuriated men skilled in the use of arms," the article reads.

Still, the *American Volunteer* called on the newly elected borough council to at least take responsibility for the source of the trouble and shut down "those dens of iniquity, the brothels and low groggeries and dance halls of Louther Street." The newspaper stated that half the crime in Carlisle could be traced to that part of town, including many arsons, robberies, riots and murders:

> *There may be lawless characters amongst some of the transient troops at the barracks, but it will not do to shut our eyes to the fact that we are under a perfect reign of terror from the lawlessness in our own midst. The wickedness of this town is notorious throughout the entire state; and we owe it to ourselves to place the strong hand of the law upon the offenders, and to vindicate the character of the community.*

As for the army, Grier confined his troops to the post. This stopped the trouble in town but did not improve discipline among the ranks. On April 17, 1868, a large number of soldiers held a meeting in which they drafted a list of demands to present to the commandant, calling for fewer restrictions along with better food and quarters. Grier conducted his own investigation of the riot, which resulted in all of the soldiers escaping a court-martial after they denied involvement in the incident. Within days of presenting his report, Grier was relieved of command and replaced by Brigadier General J.P. Hatch on May 25, 1868.

PART V

A TASTE OF MALICE

Depending on the recipe, murder can be bittersweet or just plain delicious. The most innocent-looking food or beverage can make for the rudest indigestion, especially when the poison is spiked with just the right blend of greed and jealousy. On the menu today is a lethal love triangle, a toxic conspiracy, a contest of wills and the inventive use of some handy candy to conceal evidence of a crime. You will read how a scheming servant girl and a crooked, abusive businessman finally get their just desserts, while two wealthy spinsters and an innocent couple end up in the grave.

THE BITTER BREAD OF JEALOUSY: THE CASE OF SARAH CLARK

It was arsenic that murdered a dream but spared the man for greater fortune. Andrew Carothers was nineteen years old when the serving girl, Sarah Clark, poisoned his family with tainted bread. Her target was his sister, Ann, but it was their parents, John and Mary, who died and along with them his goal of being a cabinetmaker. The poison ravaged his system, crippling his limbs and leaving his hands chronically swollen. All those years of learning the trade were gone. Rendered unfit for the job, Andrew could have given up.

Instead, the young man turned his life to book learning and the pursuit of knowledge. In 1802, he became a law student under Carlisle attorney David Watts and, three years later, was admitted to the Cumberland County

Bar. Andrew Carothers achieved status among his contemporaries, who ranked him among the best lawyers in Pennsylvania. Conway Wing, in his *History of Cumberland County*, wrote how "purity of character," the "unlimited disposition of charity" and a "love of justice" made Carothers a success.

Before his death on July 26, 1836, Carothers was elected president of town council, became an elder of a local Presbyterian church and was active as a trustee, promoting the interests of his alma mater, Dickinson College. He had taken tragedy and turned it into triumph. But his story really begins with a distorted love triangle.

Sarah Clark was a servant of the Douglas family, who lived along Hoges Run near where it flows into the Conodoguinet Creek in present-day Silver Spring Township. Clark was in love with young John Douglas, but the object of her affection was more interested in Ann Carothers, who lived on the opposite shore of Hoges Run. Clark thought that if the competition were eliminated, she might have a chance with John Douglas, so she left the Douglas family and landed a job as a servant in the Carothers household.

Having nothing against the family, Clark bided her time, waiting for months for the perfect opportunity to only poison Ann, but it never came. Desperate, Clark put arsenic into a pot of leaven, which was then made into bread for the whole family. Everyone who ate a slice became sick.

The father, John Carothers, died on February 26, 1798, and was buried at the Silver Spring Meetinghouse. The *Carlisle Gazette* reported how a large number of friends and acquaintances from far away attended the funeral "to testify their regret at the loss of a man respectable for his social and domestic qualities." The wife, Mary Carothers, lingered on until June 3, 1798, and was buried beside her husband. The same newspaper noted that she possessed "all the virtues calculated to promote domestic happiness being a dutiful [wife], an affectionate mother, a good neighbor."

Ann Carothers survived this attempt on her life but was soon subjected to another dose of poison by Clark, who was ministering at her sickbed. This second attempt failed, and a partially recovered Ann went away to stay with a nearby cousin. But she was still in danger; Clark gained access to the dwelling and mixed yet another dose of arsenic in with the butter crock. Only this time, Clark was caught in the act with arsenic still in her possession after neighbors who came to help the family became sick after eating some of the butter. The neighbors survived.

By June 12, 1798, Clark was a murder suspect in county jail. She would later confess her crime to James McCormick, a local justice of the

The tombstones of Mary and John Carothers in the Silver Spring Presbyterian Church graveyard, Silver Spring Township. *Photo by Joseph Cress.*

peace. Her trial was held that October in Carlisle, and she was convicted of first-degree murder. The following August, she was sentenced to death by hanging.

Sarah Clark went to the gallows on the east end of Carlisle on October 30, 1799. Hers was the first public hanging of a woman in Cumberland County. She was attended by two German clergymen and appeared remorseful and resigned to her fate.

"POLITICAL CLARIFICATION": THE CASE AGAINST PAUL SCHOEPPE

The hotel room in which the spinster lay dying felt very closed off—unpleasant to be inside until the door was left open, allowing fresh air to circulate. Mary Parker watched as the old woman struggled. Her breathing was heavy and noisy, like a snore every time she exhaled. Her forehead felt cold, clammy and unnatural, leaving Parker to wonder how Maria Steinnecke could slip so far in just a matter of hours.

The Mansion House hotel once stood at the southwest corner of South Pitt and West High Streets in Carlisle. It is now the Safe Harbour homeless shelter.

A fellow guest of the Mansion House in Carlisle, Parker had seen the wealthy spinster at breakfast the morning of January 27, 1869. She appeared in good health then, but that changed when Steinnecke missed dinner and Parker went to visit her room. She found the woman completely prostrate in bed. The next morning, at just 6:00 a.m., Parker felt unease at seeing Steinnecke insensible, but at least the future prosecution witness could breathe easier with the door open.

Parker would later testify during the trial to seeing the alleged murderer about noon on January 28, 1869. She had asked Paul Schoeppe whether it was true what the spinster had told her—that he had given Steinnecke something to help her sleep the day before. Parker thought it strange how the German doctor reacted by vigorously shaking his head and saying "No" over and over again. Why was he suddenly so nervous?

On the witness stand, Dr. A.J. Herman testified that he was summoned to the hotel room by Schoeppe, personal physician to Steinnecke. The defendant wanted to know whether it was appropriate to bleed the old woman of the bad humors coursing through her system. Herman thought that Steinnecke was beyond this accepted medical practice of the time. He was also convinced that a stomach pump would kill the woman.

Indeed, by the time Herman had arrived, there was no detectable pulse in either wrist, and the "mushy" woman with the "crooked face" was lying on her left side practically comatose. Maria Steinnecke, age seventy, died hours later at 6:15 p.m. on January 28, 1869. At first, people thought it was death by natural causes. She did have palsy. Her body was released for burial in her hometown of Baltimore.

Suspicions of foul play began to surface, prompted by Schoeppe's own actions. The day after Steinnecke died, he presented a check drawn on her account to Lewis A. Smith, a local bank teller who questioned the validity of her alleged signature. Smith testified that the handwriting on the check more closely resembled the signature of the defendant than the victim.

There was also the matter of the last will and testament of Steinnecke, who left behind an estate worth about $45,000—the equivalent in 2009 of $716,477. A distant relative named John Rheem had arrived at the hotel room just before she died. He was tasked with recovering the paperwork that she had stashed away in a trunk. Inside was a large envelope marked as her will and dated November 17, 1868.

A local attorney read the will aloud to witnesses, who would later testify that Schoeppe was surprised by how the document divided her estate among various religious and charitable organizations. One witness told jurors that Schoeppe threw up his hands and asked "Is it possible? Is it possible? Is that all?"

Within days, Schoeppe and his attorney would go before a probate court in Baltimore and present what they claimed was her final will dated December 3, 1868. That document appointed Schoeppe sole executor of the will and bequeathed her entire estate to her doctor in Carlisle.

Naturally, the executors named in the November will challenged Schoeppe, who admitted that the December will was written in his own handwriting and that he had named as witnesses both himself and his father, a local minister. They believed that the signature of Steinnecke on the December document was either a forgery or coerced by Schoeppe exercising undue influence over the victim. They agreed that while the spinster was thinking about changing her will, there were no indications she intended on leaving the doctor all of her possessions.

All of this suspicion prompted the probate court to order the body be exhumed on February 10, 1869, and examined for any sign of foul play. The stomach was removed and analyzed by Dr. William E. Aiken, a chemistry professor at the University of Maryland, who found a trace amount of prussic acid in her body and determined that Steinnecke had been poisoned. Schoeppe was arrested on February 16 and remanded to county prison, charged with murder. His trial began on May 24.

One prosecution theory was that Schoeppe used a combination of prussic acid and morphine to murder Steinnecke. Local druggist Charles Worthington testified to selling Schoeppe a glass stopper containing half an ounce of dilated prussic acid on January 19, 1869. A medicine for nerve disorders, prussic acid has a smell like bitter almond or peach leaves. Schoeppe also purchased some morphine from Worthington.

Dollie Turner, a local chambermaid, testified to seeing Schoeppe between 10:00 and 11:00 a.m. on January 27, 1869. She told jurors that Steinnecke asked her to bring a spoon up to her room. Thurmer met Schoeppe at the door and handed him the spoon. She did not go into the room.

Herman testified that he was present during the autopsy and saw no sign of disease. He told jurors that the brain, heart, lungs and kidneys all appeared normal. On the witness stand, Herman said that he was shocked when he drew apart the victim's eyelids on the day she died and saw that her pupils were fixed and dilated. The look of her eyes reminded him of something: "The singular expression was the matter that troubled me…It put me in mind of a chicken hawk who was poisoned with a compound poison…She was overdosed with medicine."

Herman agreed that the combination of morphine and prussic acid could act as a sedative to the system. Other doctors testified that opium or one of its preparations killed Steinnecke. However, none of the witnesses at the hotel smelled an unusual odor around her body. There was even testimony to suggest that the spinster died of some other means or had even taken something herself.

One witness testified to hearing Steinnecke ask Schoeppe for something to put her to sleep, but he refused, saying that she was too weak. When the spinster said that she would take something herself, Schoeppe shook his finger at her and told her not to before leaving the room.

Hotel guest C.L. Lochman testified that those attending to Steinnecke searched her room hoping to find a clue about what may have caused her symptoms. They found a half-empty bottle of sulfuric ether on the table by her bed and a bottle of liquor on the mantle. The room smelled of disinfectant.

Defense attorneys sought to debunk the theory that prussic acid, morphine or a combination caused her death. They called as an expert witness

Dickinson College professor Charles Francis Himes, who pointed out flaws in the methods Aiken used to arrive at the cause of death. Defense witnesses also testified that based on prior cases, there was no way Steinnecke could have survived for hours the effects of prussic acid poisoning. She would have died in a fraction of the time. The *Carlisle Herald* reported in detail the closing statement made by defense attorney William H. Miller:

> *The Commonwealth has been rambling wildly over the whole field of poisons, assisted by the guesses of physicians to find a cause of death. Nature's laws are certain, but man's knowledge is limited. As the laws of Nature are harmonious, all branches of science must approach to absolute certainty although that can not be attained because of the imperfections of man.*

Defense attorney Samuel Hepburn also went after the prosecution theory: "In my whole experience, I have never seen a case tried as this has been. We appear to be called upon to prove our innocence and the Commonwealth appears to be relieved from that rule which requires it to establish our guilt… We do not quarrel with science, but we do quarrel with those who prove themselves behind the times in matters of science."

Lawyers for the defense also objected to the prosecution claim that Schoeppe was in dire need of money. The Commonwealth introduced as evidence a letter dated November 1, 1868, from Schoeppe to Steinnecke. In it, the defendant alluded to his need for money to close a real estate deal with Dr. Herman, who planned to leave Carlisle. Schoeppe explained how Herman had offered him his medical practice if he agreed to buy three homes in the borough for a total of $5,000. Herman was asking for $2,000 upfront, with the rest of the money payable in four years. The *Carlisle Herald* quoted the letter:

> *As a friend, I will tell you I will make a very successful business if I had sufficient money…Out of his books, which I have looked in, I have seen that his practice brings him in $10,000 a year. If I could hold only half of his practice, I would make well and good $5,000 a year…But for want of these $2,000, I am afraid another happier man will get this fine business. Meanwhile, I am quiet, the will of my God may be done.*

It took a jury four hours to convict Schoeppe, but the case did not end there. The defense moved for a new trial, which the judge overruled before sentencing the doctor to death by hanging. His attorneys then appealed the case to the state Supreme Court, which ultimately granted Schoeppe a new trial.

Schoeppe had powerful friends in his corner. Doctors across the country condemned the methods Aiken used to determine cause of death. The Pennsylvania Medical Society protested the verdict, along with the College of Physicians in Philadelphia and the medical societies of Cumberland, Luzerne and Allegheny Counties.

Pennsylvania's large German population rallied behind their countryman. Schoeppe received support from German-language newspapers, German politicians and German doctors from Philadelphia. His case drew so much international attention that the Prussian ambassador visited Pennsylvania governor John Greary, who wanted to run for president.

With such mounting pressure to intervene, Greary caved on December 14, 1869, by suspending the death warrant on Schoeppe pending what he called "political clarification." A special act of the state legislature authorized Cumberland County to retry the case in September 1872. This lead to the acquittal of Schoeppe after defense expert witnesses presented overwhelming evidence against the findings of Aiken.

Schoeppe left Carlisle after the verdict but within two years was imprisoned in Illinois on a forgery charge. Evidence later surfaced that Schoeppe was never formally trained as a doctor and had fled his native Prussia following a forgery conviction there.

"CRUEL AND FATAL WORK": THE DEATH OF MARY KIEHL

All went black before her eyes as Rebecca Reed collapsed to the floor. She had gone upstairs to rest at the suggestion of Mary Kiehl, who was convinced that they had been poisoned. Indeed, the eighty-one-year-old widow said as much, as both women "vomited dreadfully." It had to have been the morning coffee.

Reed would later testify that she had visited Kiehl the evening of May 27, 1879, to cure the old spinster of the fever. The North Middleton Township woman had complained to Reed of not feeling well after she fell down the cellar stairs and hurt herself. Reed stayed the night and went downtown to market the next morning. By the time she had returned between 8:00 and 9:00 a.m., breakfast was partially prepared on the stove, and a pot of coffee had already been made. Reed finished the preparations, and both women sat down to enjoy the meal.

"After I drank the second swallow, I felt sick and faint," Reed said at trial. Going into the garden, Reed passed through an opening in the fence and into the lane, where she vomited severely. She returned to the Kiehl house to find the old woman just as sick. While Kiehl insisted on Reed going upstairs to bed, Reed wanted to send for a physician. Kiehl objected, saying that they just needed some recovery time. It was 3:00 p.m. before Reed decided it was time to leave.

"I sat on the floor awhile and laid my head on a chair," Reed said, recalling what happened upstairs. "Mary came up and laid down. I came down as soon as I felt able and started for home." Reed testified that before she left, Kiehl told her that the coffee had been prepared by Catharine Zell, a neighbor who lived only four or five houses away.

Reed did not get far before she had to vomit again. She continued to feel sick until the next morning. Kiehl would die two days later under enough suspicious circumstances for authorities to exhume her body from the Carlisle Springs Cemetery on June 6, 1879.

During the autopsy, Dr. S.B. Kieffer removed the stomach, tying it off at both ends to preserve its contents. He placed the organ along with two sections of intestines into a jar. The doctor also removed sections of the liver, which were placed in a separate jar. Authorities then turned over the evidence to W.F. Horn, a local druggist, who confirmed that the specimens tested positive for trace amounts of arsenic.

At trial, Kieffer testified that his examination of the internal organs turned up signs of inflammation. He ruled the death violent and not one caused by any disease he knew. Investigators removed two coffeepots from the Kiehl residence, which also tested positive for trace amounts of arsenic.

Investigators soon identified Zell as a suspect, along with William Wynkoop, Kiehl's business agent. The prosecution's theory was that Wynkoop provided the arsenic that Zell used to poison the widow. There was speculation that the suspects were lovers who had conspired to commit the murder. The court convened separate trials against Zell and Wynkoop.

Reed, who emerged as the key prosecution witness, testified that she was walking to Kiehl's home when she saw Zell leave with a little tin cup in her hand. Zell told Reed that she had just been up to visit the widow and brought her some beef, coffee and crackers.

Reed testified that she next saw Zell days after Kiehl's death. Reed recalled saying how shocked she was that the widow was dead and that both she and the victim got sick on the coffee. Zell admitted she had taken what remained of the coffee home and used it but did not get sick. Zell also told Reed that Kiehl had vomited so badly the day of her death that Zell did not know whether to give salts to stop the nausea. When Reed asked Zell why she didn't send for a doctor, Zell responded that Kiehl had insisted that God almighty was her doctor and she didn't want any mortal physician.

Zell's attorney argued that she had no motive to poison Kiehl and that her presence in the old widow's home was just a show of neighborly kindness. Two women testified that the victim and the accused were on friendly terms and that Kiehl had visited Zell frequently. The defense also called several witnesses in support of its theory that the death was a suicide and not a criminal act.

William Sheaffer testified that in late 1875 Kiehl came to live with his daughter for three months and that the old widow seemed to be in trouble. Greatly agitated, Kiehl said on three different occasions that she saw no other way and had nothing to live off anymore. She would sometimes sit and complain about how she was being treated by her daughter and son-in-law.

Another witness, Sarah Nickey, testified that she would often talk to Kiehl at Zell's house and that the widow seemed to be in trouble all the time. Frequently, Kiehl would say that if things didn't go better she would put herself out of the way. A third witness, Joseph Ebright, talked to Kiehl in her garden about three to four weeks before her death. The window complained about how she was being mistreated by her daughters and was having problems with Wynkoop.

The prosecution argued that while Zell was guilty of the murder, Wynkoop was an accessory before the fact because he had obtained the poison and had persuaded Zell to commit the crime. Though not at the scene, this would make Wynkoop just as guilty.

Testimony established that Kiehl had put Wynkoop in charge of her money and had given him power of attorney to transact her business. Following an argument she had with her daughter, she made Wynkoop executor of her estate, leaving to him in her will property valued at about $2,000, compared to $5 for her daughter. However, shortly before her death, Kiehl told people of her plans to change her will because she had reconciled with her daughter.

Witnesses said that Kiehl became dissatisfied with how Wynkoop was handling her money and even accused the suspect of defrauding her. It was claimed that Wynkoop, without her knowledge, had used her money to buy her house and change the name on the deed to "Amanda Wynkoop," his wife. Wynkoop admitted to taking $500 to $600 worth of her gold and silver and selling it without her approval.

Kiehl wanted all of her property out of his hands, leading the prosecution to theorize that the suspect had the old widow poisoned before she could take steps to revoke the will or rescind his fiscal responsibility. Ultimately, a jury acquitted Wynkoop of the murder charge, and the probate court ended up granting him possession of the Kiehl home.

As for Zell, the prosecution argued that since she had waited on Kiehl until the widow died, Zell had ample opportunity to continue to administer the poison. No other person attended to Kiehl or had given her anything to eat or drink, nor was a physician or a relative called to her bedside. Since much of the case rested on the testimony of Reed, the defense called eighteen witnesses to dispute her honesty, while the prosecution countered with seventeen witnesses who testified that she had a good reputation.

The prosecution also claimed that a package of arsenic was planted as false evidence in the Kiehl home to cast suspicions on Reed. Testimony was given showing the similarity in handwriting between Zell and the name "Rebecca Reed" written on the package that had been purchased from a local drugstore.

Benjamin Long testified to seeing Zell and Amanda Wynkoop at the victim's home after the widow had died and the probate court had awarded William Wynkoop ownership of the property. Long told the jury that the women found a package labeled "arsenic" in a box labeled "notions and scraps" under the bed. The box and its contents were turned over to Mr. Wynkoop, who then submitted the evidence to the authorities.

Relatives of Kiehl testified that they examined the box the day of the funeral and found only small bundles of scrap cloth and patches. A lab test later confirmed that the package contained arsenic. The drugstore owner testified that he sold William Wynkoop a package of arsenic in January 1876. The store label on the package matched the type of label the store had used at the time. Matthew Wynkoop, the suspect's father, testified his son had purchased the arsenic for him to use to poison rats.

Through her attorney, Zell filed a petition for a new trial in which the defense alleged that the guilty verdict was secured by holding out an inducement to some jurors that if Zell were convicted, the jury panel would sign a petition to pardon her. The judge found no evidence to suggest that this had any influence on the outcome.

The defense also argued that the court did not give due consideration to evidence discovered late in the trial in the form of a statement made by Ebright. He quoted Zell as saying to Kiehl, "We had better go for a doctor," but Kiehl said, "I don't want any doctor, Jesus is my doctor." But the judge said that little reliance could be placed on statements made in this wild way.

That December, a county judge denied her petition by saying that Zell received a fair and impartial trial with just consideration of her legal rights. He suggested that the condemned woman humble herself before God and plea for mercy in preparation for her death by hanging. Instead, Zell appealed the low court ruling to the state Supreme Court. The *Valley Sentinel* reported these words as the judge pronounced sentence:

> *The victim of your crime, though 81, was in vigorous and robust health when you, for some wicked and devilish purpose, began the destruction of her life by administering to her a most deadly poison…You persistently pressed on in your cruel and fatal work until you succeeded in the accomplishment of your purpose. No doubt you supposed your work was being done in so subtle and secret a way as that no human agency or efforts would ever discover the crime and your connection with it.*

Two months later, the Supreme Court reversed the county court ruling and granted Zell a new trial. The high court found that the county court erred in allowing Reed to testify to comments made by Kiehl when Zell was not present. The newspaper quoted the written decision: "The natural order of evidence should have been to receive the prisoner's admission first and afterward the statements of the deceased to Reed. It has grown into a habit these few years for counsel to propose a chain of evidence, the first links of which depend on those that follow and would not be competent without them. The court should keep a wary eye."

The prosecution was not allowed to present this hearsay testimony in a second trial, which received very little newspaper coverage. The subsequent acquittal of Zell by a different jury was considered a foregone conclusion, drawing hardly the same excitement as the first trial.

"A STRUGGLE FOR SUPREMACY": THE CANDY MAN CADAVER

It must have been unnerving for James Garjulakos when the man he suspected of murder wished him "Good morning" and offered him a soda. The Greek immigrant feared for his life and wondered if Angelo Tornatore was capable of further violence. Then came Annie Pishotta and her offer to him to join them for breakfast. No doubt Garjulakos, the only witness to the crime, thought that she may be just as willing to kill as her brother. No surprise, he refused both invitations, made early on April 13, 1909.

From 1:30 a.m. to 5:30 a.m., Garjulakos sat wide awake and terrified in his second-floor room in Carlisle, wondering if he would be next to die. He had heard the struggle between Tornatore and John Pishotta, followed by something heavy being moved downstairs. Then there were the sounds of running water, frantic scrubbing and multiple trips between the floors of the West High Street home. A boarder, he could see shadows moving in the room next door through a quarter-inch hole in the partition wall. He would later testify to hearing the hushed voices of people whom he believed to be the siblings talking to each other.

For four hours, Garjulakos stayed by the locked door that he had barricaded with furniture, cautious not to make a sound as he held in his hand the unlit kerosene lamp that he intended to use as a weapon should anyone storm the room. At one point, Tornatore jangled the knob and knocked on the door, wondering if Garjulakos was awake. It was shocking enough for Garjulakos to be roused from slumber by the sound of two gunshots followed by a loud thud and a man groaning.

Garjulakos only left his room at about 6:00 a.m. and went outside to open the shoeshine booth that he operated in front of the combination candy store, fruit stand and ice cream parlor owned by the Pishottas. He didn't know what to do at first and was afraid to say anything to anyone. Tornatore had opened the business at 8:00 a.m. when he greeted Garjulakos and offered him the soda. This so unnerved Garjulakos that he would later cross the street to the Mansion House hotel, where he tipped a colored boy to retrieve his coat from his room. Garjulakos then reported his suspicions to police.

Officers were on the scene within minutes and asked Mrs. Pishotta the whereabouts of her husband. The Italian immigrant said she didn't know, but Police Chief Daniel Fought was unconvinced. He ordered his men to search the property, at which they found signs of foul play.

Here and there, police saw blood droplets and places where the wallpaper had been scrubbed so hard that some of the coloring had come off. There was a bloody handprint on an upstairs dresser along with blood around a bedroom door and downstairs in the basement. Police also found bloodstained clothes under the cellar stairs, along with a large belt buckle, a melted pair of eyeglasses and the remains of a set of suspenders among the ash and burnt coals of the furnace.

Chief Fought stepped on something as he walked around the dark basement. He struck a match to take a closer look, only to find a man's coat

This photograph of the first block of West High Street in Carlisle shows the crime scene on the far right as the Monyer's Restaurant, later the Peerless Candy Company.

and bloodstained shirt. Fought also saw a hole in the floor about six feet square and six feet deep. When he reached over to touch a corner, Fought felt something like a man's head. Police had found the body of John Pishotta, sitting with his back against the wall of a vault or wine cellar and with one leg partly raised. Stone, brick and mortar covered almost his entire body.

The body was carried upstairs to a room that the victim had used as a five-cent theatre and, more recently, an ice cream parlor. There, investigators conducted an autopsy, which found evidence of severe trauma to the top of the head along with defensive wounds. One finger on his left hand was cut almost to the bone. But the fatal injury was an inch-and-a-half-deep cut to the throat extending from the right ear to below the lower jaw. This clean cut by a very sharp instrument severed both the windpipe and an artery, causing the victim to bleed out and die within five minutes. What was found at the scene was enough to convince police to arrest Annie Pishotta and her brother Tornatore. Ironically, this was not the first time John Pishotta had been the subject of a police investigation.

A Taste of Malice

Murder victim John Pishotta can be seen buried under rubble.

The victim had once served eighteen months in an Ohio state prison for trying to bribe a jury in a murder trial involving his brother, who was accused of killing a police officer. John Pishotta was also accused of kidnapping the four-year-old son of a business partner and then taking the child to the boy's mother in Italy. That case was never prosecuted because Pishotta had made no effort to collect a ransom and had released the boy unharmed.

There was mention of a troubled marriage in the newspaper reports and that John was so abusive to Annie that she had consulted with a Harrisburg attorney, who instructed her to scold her husband. There was even speculation in the press that Annie Pishotta and Tornatore were lovers and that, years before, she had tipped police on the whereabouts of her fugitive husband, leading to his eventual imprisonment.

Natives of Sicily, the couple once lived in Washington, Pennsylvania, where Annie had a candy business while her husband learned to make candy. While he served time in Ohio, Annie rejoined relatives in Italy for about six months before returning to the United States. She then moved to Carlisle in October 1905, where she purchased the Frank Farabelli confectioner business on High Street.

Annie then established the Peerless Candy Company, identifying her husband on legal documents as George B. Pishotta, which was the alias he had used as a fugitive. Upon release from prison, John Pishotta joined his wife in Carlisle but still wanted to help his brother by asking her for money so he could bribe the watchman at the prison holding his brother. When Annie refused, John decided not to speak to her out of protest.

That apparently changed the evening of April 12, 1909, when husband and wife talked about the success of the Easter receipts, which totaled about $380 (the equivalent of $8,933 in 2008).

The night of the murder, John Pishotta went into his bedroom and demanded money from his wife, but again she refused him. So he grabbed her, slapped her in the face and pointed a revolver at her. She ran downstairs into the kitchen screaming in Italian "My mother, he's going to kill me." John ran after her with the gun in his hand. The commotion woke up Tornatore, who had been living in the house just over a month. Hearing his sister in distress, he rushed to her aid, grabbing a straight razor as he left his room. He found the couple in the first-floor kitchen.

Annie and her brother were to be tried separately in county court, with his trial scheduled first. Tornatore testified that he killed John Pishotta out of self-defense and then, ashamed of his actions, tried to conceal the body and the evidence from his sister. She testified to playing no role in the murder or the attempt by her brother to hide the crime. Annie said that she only became aware of her husband's death after her arrest.

Tornatore testified that he opened the kitchen door and saw John with the gun. When Pishotta wheeled around, Tornatore closed the door as John fired the first shot. Tornatore crouched down and opened the door again, only to push it shut just as Pishotta fired the second shot. At that point, Tornatore decided to make a grab for the gun by rushing John Pishotta, who had turned his back to the door.

Annie testified how she ran out of the house and had fainted in the yard after hearing gunfire. She woke up sometime later but stayed outside until daybreak, when she figured it was safe to reenter. When she asked her brother "Where is John?", Tornatore told her that he fled after the fight.

During the struggle for the gun, Tornatore slashed Pishotta several times with the razor, including one cut across the front of the neck. This caused John Pishotta to loosen his grip on the gun enough for Tornatore

The basement of the Peerless Candy Company, where police found the body in the rectangular hole.

to seize the revolver and slam it into his brother-in-law's head. On his way down, Pishotta's head hit the sink and floor, causing a fractured skull. The newspaper reported his testimony: "The struggle was terrible; beyond human comprehension. It was just a fight which, in one second or another, it would decide death...It was a struggle for supremacy."

Seeing Pishotta down, Tornatore ran upstairs to get some towels to put under John's head, only to realize that the man had passed away. He would testify to spending frantic moments scrubbing the walls and floor. He even plugged the bullet holes in the kitchen door with candy paste and then painted it over.

Tornatore said that the whole time he felt dizzy and trembled and that there was a cold sweat on his forehead. He did not want his sister to view the crime scene, so he had to work quickly. In his haste to conceal the body, Tornatore tripped and fell into the subchamber, dragging the body with him.

The trial of Angelo Tornatore lasted six days. In the end, the jury deliberated his fate for four hours before finding him not guilty of murder based on self-defense. The acquittal prompted the prosecution to drop its case against Annie Pishotta, and she was found not guilty by a different jury. The newspaper was there to record the emotion felt by those in the audience and the defendant's family:

> *Frank Tornatore threw his arms around the neck of Angelo and kissed him repeatedly and refused to release his embrace. All at once, he became hysterical and threw his arms toward the jury and said "Hurrah for American men." All the women sobbed audibly and went up to Angelo, who was also sobbing. Angelo then arose and, addressing the jury, said between sobs "I thank you for the sincere and judicious judgment you gave in my behalf. In this supreme moment, I wish to shake hands with all of you."*

The crime scene did not last long enough for an encore. The owners soon realized that all the publicity around the murder made it impossible to rent out the rooms, so the building was demolished that summer to make way for the Orpheum Theater. This popular entertainment venue was, in turn, destroyed by fire in 1938.

The original building was once the home of James Hamilton Jr., a well-known local land speculator, lawyer, scientist and political leader of the 1800s. One provision of Hamilton's will was a $2,000 bequest to Cumberland County for the development of what was to become the historical society on North Pitt Street. This nonprofit organization acquired the land on which the murder scene used to sit during an expansion program in the 1990s. A parking lot now covers the subchamber vault in which the body of John Pishotta was found.

PART VI

COLD CASES AND TRIALS BY FIRE

The book ends with an overview of other notorious murder cases of the twentieth century. I start with Prohibition and a budding young romance brought to a sudden and tragic end by a killer whose identity remains a mystery. I then turn to the ravings of a madman whose rampage one scorching hot August day had a profound impact on courthouse security. I then touch on the dubious career and nefarious end of a local madam and her whorehouse. Finally, the book closes just as it had begun, with a rude awakening to mayhem brewing just beneath the surface.

"Lead Kindly Light": The Moonshine Murders

Here and there, Joseph Ganster caught signs of his son's passing. The worried father used a flashlight to follow the tire treads on the muddy road leading away from the Limit, a hunting camp at the base of the mountain. Twenty-year-old Harry Ganster had gone this way, along with his twenty-one-year-old girlfriend, Leah Ellenberger, to pick flowers for his upcoming graduation from Marysville Area High School. Joseph Ganster had suggested that his son search the area beyond the camp, fully expecting Harry to return home by nightfall as promised. But the couple never showed up, so the father enlisted the help of George Albright, Leah's uncle, to try and find them. At first, they had no luck, and concern was mounting.

Both men scanned the edges of the narrow, steep road that wound its way up the slope. They saw where the couple stopped long enough to pluck honeysuckle and dogwood blossoms direct from the vine. Travel was difficult, as the path moved over broken terrain, but finally the men reached the summit and spotted the car pulled over to the side of the road in Lamb's Gap about three miles north of Hogestown and only forty feet from the Perry County line.

"What's going on here?" the father shouted. Peering into the darkness, Ganster could see his son leaning out the side of the car—his right foot on the running board, his left foot on the ground. The father figured that the boy was tired and had fallen asleep. Walking up to the car, Ganster reached out to rouse his son awake only to draw away in shock. His son was dead. His body was cold, with his left hand on the seat and his right hand on the floor beside his head. What had happened?

The girl was also dead, slumped behind the steering wheel with her head thrown back over the rear of the seat. Her left hand was resting on the driver's side door. Ganster guarded the bodies while Albright returned to Marysville to report the crime to friends, family and the authorities. Police investigators found a knife and a first-aid kit on the front seat between the victims. A finger of Harry Ganster was freshly bandaged, leading police to believe that the young man had cut himself while picking flowers.

Dr. H.H. Longsdorf of Centerville performed the autopsy. He concluded that a single bullet from a high-powered rifle killed both victims because only one ball was found and the flesh wounds on the girl were much larger than those on the boy. Longsdorf believed that the bullet struck Harry in the right arm and then went through his chest from right to left, piercing his heart before leaving the body between the fifth and sixth rib. The bullet then pierced the breast of Leah and lodged beneath the flesh on the outside of the left arm near the shoulder. It was clear that the victims were shot from ambush as Harry was entering the car. The couple probably lived for no more than five minutes.

The *Evening Sentinel* reported how the families held very different funerals in Marysville, where Harry and Leah were known as sweethearts. His service at a local evangelical church was "crowded to the doors," while hers was held at her uncle's house on Front Street and was only attended by immediate family members. The newspaper explained how Leah's mother had a breakdown upon learning of her death and was bedridden for days: "There was no music, at the request of the parents, but the dead girl's favorite hymn, 'Lead Kindly Light' was to be recited…In the large collection of floral sprays and emblems in the Albright home was one beautiful tribute from the choir of the Methodist Church."

The caskets bearing the remains of the two young sweethearts were surrounded with flowers. While classmates escorted his body to a cemetery outside town, her body was taken a few miles upriver to Duncannon, where she was buried. Students of the Marysville high school attended Harry's funeral as a group and lowered the flag to half-mast as a tribute to their senior class president.

Harry Ganster did not dance, play billiards or attend parties like his classmates. Instead, he took hikes in the mountains around town or went on car trips through the rolling hills. A young man of faith, Ganster attended church regularly on Sunday, along with prayer meetings on Wednesday. Harry was planning to attend Susquehanna University in the fall.

As for Leah Ellenberger, she was from Hollidaysburg and had recently completed a term as a teacher in West Virginia. She was known for her singing voice. The day before her death, she had taken the starring role in an amateur production presented by the Marysville high school. Frequently, while visiting Marysville, Ellenberger would sing with the Methodist church choir and had planned to perform that coming Sunday.

Harry and Leah met two years prior when she was visiting relatives in Marysville. They were often seen together cruising in his car or attending summer events in and around town. Both loved the outdoors.

The day of the murder, Leah practiced music from 1:00 p.m. to 4:00 p.m. at her aunt's house. Harry left his home at about 4:30 p.m. saying that he would be back in time for supper at 6:00 p.m. He then walked half a block to the Albright home where Leah waited with her friend, a Mrs. William Keller. The trio got into his car and drove to the Keller home. The couple invited Keller to join them on their flower hunting expedition, but she did not accompany them. She was probably the last person, outside the murderer, who saw the couple alive.

Homicide investigators advanced several theories, including that Harry was shot by moonshiners out for revenge. Two years before the murders, the teenager furnished police with photographs of stills and other information on illegal activity on the mountain. Schoolmates told authorities that Harry had been in the habit of carrying a revolver because he believed that criminals were after him. His brother, Clinton Ganster, claimed that there was evidence that moonshiners had threatened Harry's life.

Indeed, the murder took place in one of the wildest parts of the Blue Ridge chain in an area known for its manufacture of liquor. Some discounted the theory—no one knew of the trip to pick flowers, so how could they wait in ambush? Some believed that moonshiners may have seen Harry near their haunt again and followed him. After a week of hard work by his investigative team, Major Lynn Adams dismissed this theory—one of the strongest in the case—because there had been no active stills in the immediate vicinity of the crime scene for the past year.

Another theory was that Ganster was mistaken for someone else by a Marysville man who suspected his wife of adultery. She was seen taking car rides through the mountains in the company of another man. There was no evidence to prove this theory because the jealous husband was never found. However, police came across some tantalizing clues of a possible meeting place or "post office" for a local couple.

A Marysville man named Victor Fenical was searching the crime scene for bullets when he came across two notes hidden beneath a flat rock. The record is vague on the content of the notes, but one was believed to have been written by a woman, the other by a man. One note was in ink, the other in pencil. Both were hastily written in an "irregular hand" and were later classified as having no bearing on the case.

Police also investigated whether Ganster and Ellenberger were victims of a stray bullet fired by a hunter. Officers asked the hunter involved in the accidental shooting to come forward, but no one ever did. There were some clues to back up this theory, but nothing conclusive.

A nearby resident, visiting the crime scene, told police that he had heard two gunshots fired just after a Boy Scout troop had passed by his dwelling moving toward their camp near where the murders took place. He first heard the Scouts give a cheer, and then as the echo died out, he heard the first shot. This was followed by a second cheer and a second shot fired as though in salute.

Joe Sandine, also a nearby resident, told police that the gunfire in Lambs Gap may point to an armed maniac. A few years ago, his brother, John, was in the same section of the mountain as the slain couple when he was wounded in the chest by a mysterious bullet.

Yet another theory was that the murder was committed by a jilted lover of Leah's who was jealous of the attention Harry was paying the girl. At one point, investigators were seeking a Pennsylvania Railroad employee from Hollidaysburg who was seen there on Friday, the day of the crime. This man allegedly made no secret of his rage over the love affair of Harry and Leah.

Mr. Ellenberger took exception to this theory. "That is ridiculous," he told the *Evening Sentinel*. "Leah never has had a sweetheart in

Hollidaysburg. Harry is the first boy she ever went around with a great deal. Leah is just a child. She was very quiet and reserved and did not go out much. Those policemen would have you believe that she was having all kinds of love affairs."

None of the theories amounted to an arrest, and this case remains unsolved. None of the clues seemed to yield any evidence pointing to a specific suspect.

An anonymous letter received by Joseph Ganster was written and mailed by someone who knew nothing of the slaying. A crude drawing found among Harry's effects was a warning given to him two years ago by another boy who did not want the victim to take sides against a certain organization. An extensive search for Harry's diary turned up nothing, and a little black notebook found on his body yielded only a love poem, drawings from biology class and a map of mountain trails near where he died.

Although police went over the ground thoroughly, no other bullets or cartridges were found at the scene. When asked, Joseph Ganster said that his son had no enemies and was friendly with all his associates. Forced to discard all possible theories, Major Adams told the *Evening Sentinel* it could take years before a killer could ever be identified either by a confidant following an argument or by a deathbed confession. He had little faith in either one ever happening. And he was right.

"Magic Ball and Triggerman": The Courtroom Slaying of 1955

Percy Haines stood by calmly, not moving an inch, as the same revolver he used to shoot four people was now pointed at him. Court stenographer George Geiger had just threatened to kill Haines should he try to leave the courtroom. Their struggle was brief and violent before Geiger, a Korean War veteran, disarmed Haines, a sixty-year-old disgruntled husband and Newville area farmer.

Minutes before, Geiger had heard two rapid-fire shots before looking up to see Haines standing about three feet away pointing the gun in his direction near the west end of the courtroom. Geiger would later testify to his actions in the subsequent murder trial: "I jumped from my seat, ran around my stenotype machine and grabbed Haines. We struggled near the steps which lead to the court's bench and finally, while we were grappling with each other, I bumped my head on the railing of the jury box."

As Geiger used his hands to hold down his assailant's right arm, he shouted to an unidentified woman to hit Haines over the head. Gladys Cramer of Chambersburg obliged, picking up a heavy chair and using it to pummel her father. This attack broke his grip on the revolver, but during the struggle the gun went off accidentally. The bullet struck just above the door leading to the office of Ruth Greider, court reporter for President Judge Dale F. Shughart. Geiger would later testify, "I started toward the east end of the jury box chasing Haines and I shouted 'Halt, don't make a move' and 'If there are any bullets in this gun, I'll kill you.'"

Haines, sandy-haired and thin-faced, stood there and waited until police arrived. The *Sentinel* reported how he merely blinked when he heard the word "murder": "The expressionless Haines with the ruddy complexion appeared cool and calm as he was whisked from the courthouse through a crowd of several hundred people who gathered within seconds after they heard the shots ring out through the open windows of the courtroom."

The heat was oppressive that August 2, 1955, when violence erupted at about 12:36 p.m. Within forty-five minutes, a promising young attorney would be dead and three other victims hospitalized. When asked later why he opened fire, Haines replied, "I got a raw deal in court." County Judge Mark Garber had just completed a nonsupport hearing during which he ordered Haines to pay his estranged wife Lulu fifty dollars per month.

The *Sentinel* reported how Haines, not a bit remorseful, would blame others, and not himself, for the shooting that took the life of forty-one-year-old John Dysert Faller Jr. and injured Garber, Lulu Haines of Waynesboro and her lawyer, George Black of Chambersburg.

Murder suspect Percy Haines is led out of county jail in handcuffs on his way to the courthouse for trial.

The gunshots echo to this day in tighter courtroom security and the presence of a metal detector in the courthouse lobby. The cruel irony was that Faller had nothing to do with the nonsupport action that Lulu Haines had brought against Percy Haines. Court procedure required a local attorney to sit in as an associate counsel when a lawyer from outside the county appears in court. Black, not Faller, was in charge of interrogating witnesses on behalf of Lulu Haines.

Percy Haines took the stand in his own defense on September 23, 1955, in the very same courtroom in which the crime took place. The *Sentinel* reported how at times during his testimony Haines shouted at the top of his voice and used profanity. He claimed that his wife tried to poison him twice when they lived in Chicago and that he came to court with a gun to protect himself.

"Any human being would do what I did," Haines said. He testified that, when Garber issued the nonsupport order, "I got on fire and felt like I was burning up." Haines saw his wife get up from her seat and open her pocketbook. This prompted Haines to take action, though he continued to deny responsibility: "I thought she had a gun and was going to shoot me, so I reached in and got my gun and held it up and the judge's magic ball and the triggerman pulled it…If I had pulled the trigger, it would have been worse."

Prosecution witnesses testified that Haines suddenly leaped from his chair and whipped out a revolver from a pouch that he had sewn into his undershirt. He then stepped to the northeast corner of the counsel table and fired three shots in quick succession. The first bullet struck his wife in the abdomen. The second shot hit Faller in the upper right chest. The third shot hit Black in the upper right arm. Faller had been seated between Lulu Haines and Black.

Cramer testified that she saw her mother slump to the floor. She then witnessed her father run three steps and then fire at Garber, who was seeking protection behind the bench. Cramer picked up a chair and threw it at her father, but she was uncertain whether it struck him. When Geiger was grappling with her father for the revolver, she struck him several times on the head to help Geiger obtain the weapon.

During his testimony, Haines shouted out his recall of what happened next: "I told him [Geiger] if he had the guts to kill me. Go ahead because I got the guts to take it."

First responders found Lulu Haines stretched out on a bench toward the back of the courtroom. She was hospitalized in critical condition for four days but ultimately recovered.

Garber, meanwhile, ran into the law library, picked up a phone and called an ambulance. He then went to the jury room across the hall, where Judge

This was the courtroom of the old county courthouse shortly after the shooting. Percy Haines, along with his victims, sat at the table in the foreground.

Shughart was convening a hearing at the time of the shooting. Garber told Shughart, "I've been shot." Indeed, the bullet had shattered bone and broken blood vessels. Garber walked down the rear stairs and into Court Street, where he waited for an ambulance.

As Garber got into the ambulance, he told Shughart, "You had better go back to the courtroom. I think some other people have been shot." Shughart raced for a phone and advised the staff at Carlisle Hospital to round up every surgeon and physician possible to help care for the wounded.

As for Black, he managed to walk down the front steps of the old courthouse but collapsed just as he opened the front door, leaving behind a pool of blood. The bullet fractured his right arm, but Black also recovered to join Lulu Haines and the Faller estate in filing damage suits against Percy Haines.

Meanwhile, Faller walked out the southeast door of the courtroom before crawling on his hands and knees down the front stairs, across the main corridor and into the clerk of courts office. Bleeding profusely, his face chalk-white, Faller was semiconscious when he collapsed just inside the office door. "My God, get an ambulance and police to the courthouse," were among his last words.

An ambulance rushed Faller to Carlisle Hospital, where doctors tried in vain to save him. Faller was given blood transfusions but died at about 1:25 p.m. of pulmonary hemorrhage before emergency surgery could be done to remove the bullet that had lodged near the top of his left lung. He was a son of the late John D. Faller, a leading member of the county bar association.

John D. Faller Jr.

A 1949 Dickinson School of Law graduate, John Faller Jr. led the legal fight to save the old Market House on the Square, but ultimately that building was condemned and torn down. The modern courthouse was built on that site. A World War II veteran, Faller also served as general counsel to the Pennsylvania Turnpike Commission and as a director of the Hamilton Library Historical Association, known today as the county historical society.

Thirty-four lawyers and judges gathered in the same courtroom in which Faller was mortally wounded to eulogize and honor the memory of "a gentleman" and "scholar with high integrity." The *Sentinel* quoted Shughart as saying, "The young man stricken down in this courtroom had his career terminated when it was still in its ascendancy. He had not yet obtained his full greatness and would have grown higher in ability and wisdom had he not been cut down."

Attorney Robert Lee Jacobs said that Faller never suffered from indecision and never compromised on a case. An editorial in the *Sentinel* described the impact of the loss:

We read about such violence occurring in other places, but we ordinarily conclude it won't happen here. The sudden ending of the life and career of John D. Faller Jr. has caused a pall of sadness over the community which hangs all the more heavily because of the serious injury suffered the three others. The slayer should and he will suffer due punishment for this awful crime. There is little need to call for that for justice will take its course. Nothing, however, can blot out the tragedy.

District Attorney Clinton Weidner called for the death penalty in his case. He was challenged on this by Charles Ware, the defense counsel appointed for Haines by Judge W. Clarence Sheely of Gettysburg, who was president of the Dickinson law school board of trustees. The Pennsylvania Supreme Court appointed Sheely to serve as the presiding judge in the murder trial because both Cumberland County judges were considered witnesses in the case. Sheely also appointed John J. Snyder of New Cumberland as a defense attorney for Haines. Snyder used to live in Carlisle and had attended Dickinson School of Law.

In a plea for mercy, Ware stressed his client's paranoia, reminding the jury that Haines had suffered from mental illness since 1929, when he first accused his wife of poisoning him. Indeed, psychiatrists for both the Commonwealth and defense described Haines as the type of person who shifted blame to others but knew right from wrong, was conscious of his acts and was capable of planning such a crime. The *Sentinel* reported the following from Ware's closing statement: "I fully feel that this man is sick in his mind that he is not fully responsible for what took place in this very courtroom…Here's a man who did a terrible thing…but I think his mind was so disordered that he was not entirely responsible for this horrible tragedy. I know he has to be punished but I hope you will spare his life."

On the witness stand, Haines held fast to the claim the "judge's magic ball and the triggerman" fired the four shots that killed Faller and wounded three others. But Weidner punched holes in his story during cross-examination. While Haines testified to seeing his wife open her pocketbook as if to reach for a gun, he also admitted that she was moving away from the table at the time of the shooting and that he never knew her to own a gun. Haines also testified that his wife made no threats to him in the last eleven years nor did he ever complain to police about any attempts by her to take his life.

But perhaps the most damaging piece of evidence against Haines was a statement he made and signed less than two hours after being taken into custody. In it, Haines wrote "I got mad" and that he shot his wife because

A sketch drawing of
Percy Haines testifying
during the trial.

he feared she was out to get rid of him. The statement went on to read
how Haines shot Faller because he was defending a "no good woman"
and Black because of a "crooked deal a couple years ago." The newspaper
accounts did not elaborate. As for Garber, Haines wrote how he was upset at
receiving such an unjust decision after telling the judge that his court had no
jurisdiction over him since he obtained the divorce in Reno, Nevada, back
in 1954.

Indeed, Carlisle attorney J. Boyd Landis, who represented Percy Haines
the day of the shooting, testified at the murder trial to his client's state of
mind after Garber issued the nonsupport order. Haines turned to Landis
and asked, "How can I pay when I don't have no money?" To which, Landis
replied, "We'll take care of that later." There was no later. As Landis gathered
up paperwork to put back into the file, he heard two rapid-fire shots and
turned to see his former client holding a gun. Landis escaped unhurt.

In the course of debunking his excuse, Weidner asked Haines straight up:
"Wouldn't it be important for the state police to know about the magic ball?"
The *Sentinel* reported how Haines skipped that answer and never wavered
from his denial of pulling the trigger even though he held the gun. "This
wasn't a one-man circus," Haines told the court. "I'll take my responsibility,
but let them take theirs."

In making his case, Weidner asked the jury not to base its verdict on pity or
mercy but rather on the facts, which demand the death penalty. He argued

shifting the blame to the "magic ball" and "triggerman" was just a ploy by Haines to avoid death row. Weidner described the defendant as a calculating, cunning person who was loud, boisterous and profane on the witness stand and wanted to place the blame on someone else. The *Sentinel* captured his words: "Retribution demands the death penalty here to protect society from a dangerous criminal. There is no evidence the defendant can be reformed by confinement in a prison."

Reporters covering the court proceedings consistently described Haines as being calm and collected prone to only occasional signs of worry. He was seen biting his lips, rubbing his hands together and nervously chewing gum. When asked how he wished to be tried on the charge of murder, Haines managed to reply in a soft, quivering tone, "By God and my country."

Haines was placed under tight security and twenty-four-hour suicide watch. The *Sentinel* reported how, while confined as an inmate at the county jail, Haines beat himself into unconsciousness by knocking his head against the wall and floor of his cell. This attempt at self-destruction came less than twenty-four hours after Haines was informed that he had been sued as a defendant in civil lawsuits totaling $600,000.

The jury in his murder trial deliberated for about five and a half hours before arriving at a guilty verdict—but with a surprising twist. The *Sentinel* reporter knew of at least two ballots cast resulting in an eight-to-four and a nine-to-three vote in favor of life imprisonment. The newspaper reported how Haines took on an expression of satisfaction by displaying a half grin and by shaking the hands of his court-appointed lawyers.

In passing down sentence, Sheely told Haines that he was fortunate that the jury found extenuating circumstances to recommend life imprisonment because the evidence fully justified the death penalty. When asked if he had any comment, Haines had nothing to say.

Weidner made it clear to reporters that he would exert every effort to make sure Percy Haines never returned to society. As the murder trial concluded, Haines was arrested and charged with three counts of assault with intent to kill. Haines ended up dying in state prison.

The murder of John D. Faller Jr. prompted the Pennsylvania General Assembly to launch a state police investigation into recent outbreaks of violence in courtrooms. State Representative Arthur George said that such acts of anarchy against the quiet dignity of the courtroom cannot be tolerated. He pushed for measures to prevent a recurrence of what happened in Carlisle and in Warren County in January 1954 when a litigant in a nonsupport trial shot and killed a county judge.

"Blood on Their Hands": The Murdered Madam

The whorehouse was quiet and the robber had left when Georgia Ann Schneider felt safe enough to walk downstairs from her room on the third floor to the second-floor bedroom of Bessie Jane Jones.

Schneider opened the door, looked inside and saw blood—lots of blood—from the old madam who had been stabbed to death. That was when fear of the syndicate took hold of the Pittsburgh area woman. "I wanted to get away," Schneider testified during her February 1973 murder trial. "I was very scared."

Earlier that morning of October 1, 1972, fellow prostitute Cassandra Jackson had warned Schneider to stay in her room because a man from New Kensington was coming to rob Jones. Schneider heeded the warning and waited until after the noise died down before checking on Bessie. She testified to leaving the brothel within twenty minutes of finding the body. Before going, Schneider asked Jackson not to tell anyone in the syndicate that she was at the whorehouse the morning of the stabbing: "I didn't want my family hurt."

Schneider had arrived in Carlisle the evening of September 30 to work for Jones, as she had several times in the two years prior to the murder. Her plan was to turn tricks a few more weeks before leaving for Pittsburgh to have her baby. Schneider was about six months pregnant at the time of the murder.

Borough police were first notified of the death at about 6:10 a.m. on October 1. Upon arrival at 20 East Locust Street, they found Jones on a bed in an upstairs bedroom. Someone had used a pair of nylons to tie her hands behind her back and had stuffed a washcloth in her mouth. Her nightgown, slip and housecoat were all stained with blood from three knife wounds to the left arm, left rib cage and chest. The fatal wound cut the pulmonary artery at the base of the heart, causing massive bleeding.

A third-generation madam, Jones died a legend in Carlisle. Those old enough remembered a plump old woman wearing a big floppy hat and too much makeup. As she walked downtown to market, Jones used a cane, though many suspect that it was more for show than anything else.

Her whorehouse on Locust Street catered only to high-class customers—mostly white men in positions of power including judges, generals, lawyers, police chiefs and legislators. A savvy businesswoman, Jones kept out the riffraff in favor of prominent citizens and well-to-do farmers. An oversized ledger, recovered after her death, listed the sexual

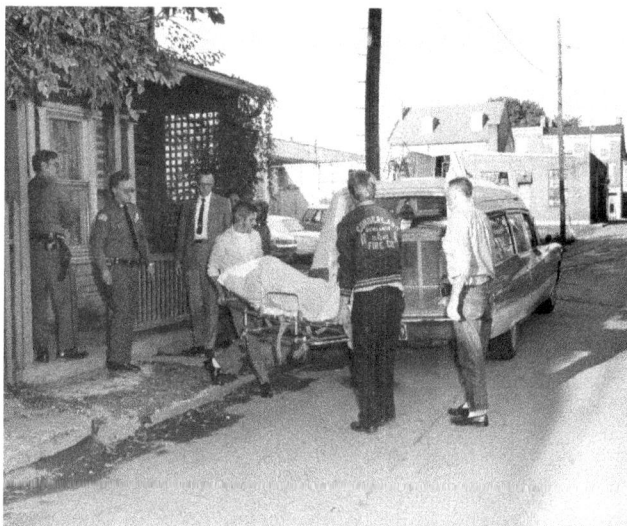

Officials remove Bessie Jones from her brothel the day of her murder.

Murder suspect Georgia Schneider, *center*, with her attorney Herbert C. Goldstein.

preferences of more than 1,600 customers from 1947 to just two days before Jones was murdered. This book has since been stashed away in a safe deposit box by the same attorney who represented her alleged killer. The madam who tried so hard in life to avoid publicity ended up being the victim of an unsolved murder case.

Carlisle police, along with the county district attorney, were convinced that Schneider was the prime suspect. A switchblade with the victim's blood was found in the yard next to a wrapper from a package of stomach medicine that Schneider admitted to have used. Jackson was the key prosecution witness during the trial of Schneider, which ended with a not guilty verdict on the murder charge.

Jackson testified that Schneider had arrived at the whorehouse at about 9:00 p.m. the night before the murder. The suspect did not work but rather came by to spend the night because she was feeling sick. Jones had asked Jackson to help Schneider into bed. That was when Schneider allegedly told Jackson of her intention to rob Jones. According to testimony by Jackson, Schneider admitted that she had robbed Jones before and was afraid Bessie would recognize her as an assailant. Jackson testified she saw a knife similar to the murder weapon in Schneider's room the morning of the murder.

Jackson last spoke to Jones between 3:00 and 3:30 a.m. on October 1, when she received a phone call and went to meet at friend at the Starlite Motel on Route 11. Jackson testified that Schneider told her that she had to use the knife after Bessie pulled out a gun. Investigators fixed the time of death at about 5:30 a.m.

Schneider left Carlisle and took a taxi to Harrisburg. Along the way, the cab driver saw her stuff money into her pants. Schneider then hailed another cab at the bus terminal and asked that driver to take her to Pittsburgh for $110. According to testimony, Schneider gave her name as "Melissa" and told the second driver, "If you can make it in good time, there's a good tip in it for you."

She also told the man to leave the dome light on in the cab so she could count the money. While he did not look back, he heard some rustling coming from the backseat. At about 7:05 a.m., police stopped this second taxi on the Pennsylvania Turnpike about twelve miles west of Carlisle.

When police arrested Schneider, they found about $2,789 on the cab seat and stuffed in her handbag and her clothing. Schneider said that she had earned the money while working as a prostitute in New York City, but the prosecution argued that her pregnancy would have reduced her value as a prostitute. Also, Schneider could not produce the address of the club in which she claimed to have worked.

Defense attorney Herbert "Corky" Goldstein said that an organized crime syndicate, possibly from Pittsburgh, was responsible for killing Jones and for several robberies leading up to the murder. It was believed that a big city syndicate supplied the prostitutes for the whorehouse. Two "girls" would come in every two weeks by bus on a Friday night from Baltimore, Pittsburgh or Philadelphia. The "girls" left two Fridays later when two other women arrived. The gaudy clothes and excessive makeup made the prostitutes easy to spot on the bus. Many local residents simply overlooked or even tolerated the whorehouse.

Goldstein argued that evidence pointed to signs of a professional hit. His client tried to call for help, but the phone lines serving the building had been cut. "This is consistent with a hired killer, but not with Georgia," Goldstein told jurors. He added that no blood was found on his client's clothing and that her fingerprints were not found on the murder weapon. "Whoever did it must have gotten some blood on their hands and on their clothing," Goldstein said. The prosecution countered that a hit man would never leave a knife behind.

Shortly before Jones's death, the *Sentinel* reported that she was under investigation by the Federal Bureau of Investigation, the state attorney general's office and state police for her alleged connections to an interstate prostitution syndicate. Indeed, her death marked the fourth time in eight months that Jones had been robbed.

On March 1, 1972, two McKeesport men were put on trial for robbery, but the case resulted in a hung jury. Two months later, on May 19, the whorehouse was ransacked by six armed men, who took cash and jewelry. At that time, Jones and three unidentified women were bound, gagged and robbed of several hundred dollars. Usually, Jones avoided reporting such incidents to police because she did not want law enforcement involved.

Goldstein speculated that the friend Jackson met at the motel before the murder might have been associated with the crime. He reminded jurors that Jackson met with a man from Pittsburgh for about forty-five minutes and that the man was last seen walking down Route 11 at about 6:00 a.m.

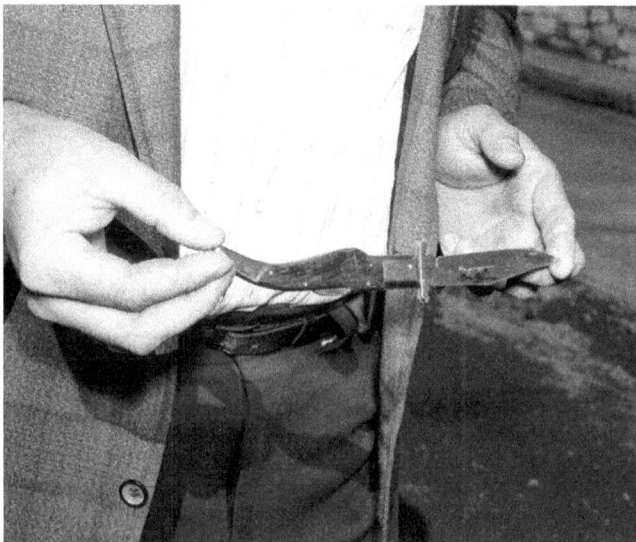

The knife found in the yard.

"Would a man come all the way from Pittsburgh just to have a conversation?" Goldstein asked.

The defense was successful. The jury found Schneider not guilty of murder and robbery. However, she was serving time in state prison for trying to escape from the Cumberland County jail at High and Bedford Streets on October 9, 1972. Schneider was apprehended about a block away by prison authorities and local police.

In June 1990, Goldstein held a press conference during which he announced how the ledger or "Preference Book" was locked away in a safe deposit box. Goldstein said that Schneider first told him of its existence four months after the murder trial while she was still serving time for the prison breach.

Goldstein told reporters that Schneider had obtained the ledger from Jones, who allegedly said, "If anything should happen, I want you to make sure this book doesn't see the light of day."

Schneider instructed a friend to give Goldstein the ledger because she did not feel safe keeping it and wanted to make sure nothing happened to it. The ledger included not only the names and each client's favorite services but also his occupation, customer rates and a record of money owed and paid.

"It was just a customer book," Goldstein said. "It was not kept to hurt anybody."

The 1990 story reported how Carlisle police were certain that Schneider had perpetrated the crime but also that she couldn't be tried again on a murder charge. Michael Eakin, district attorney at the time, said that he saw no reason to reopen the case. "The mere fact that she was acquitted does not mean she did not commit the murder," Eakin told the *Sentinel*.

Local tradition has the roots of the whorehouse going back to the Civil War, when Jane Andrews, a former slave and camp follower, arrived in Carlisle in June 1863 with the Confederate forces that had occupied the town. As the story goes, when the soldiers left for Gettysburg, Andrews stayed behind and decided to open a brothel, which was later passed down to her daughter, Cora Andrews. Historians dispute this version by pointing out that 1860 census data shows that Jane Andrews was born in Pennsylvania and was already living in Carlisle before the Civil War. Either way, Cora Andrews passed down the family business to Bessie and her sisters, Dorothy and Marion, sometime in the early 1920s.

Bessie Jones always took the necessary precautions to avoid being raided. She usually worked the door, only allowing entry to those whom she recognized. This still did not prevent an occasional raid, and between 1939

Bessie's house, showing fire damage from the 1964 arson.

and 1971, Bessie faced eight counts of operating a house of prostitution and four liquor law violations. She always seemed to weather her legal storms.

During Prohibition, her whorehouse doubled as a speakeasy at which customers could buy beer or whiskey as they waited in the parlor for the next available prostitute. In 1964, a maid named Beatrice Ahl discovered some cash inside a pillowcase. She and three men removed several thousand dollars from the house before setting it afire on January 18. Firefighters putting out the flames discovered about $45,000 hidden in a silk pillowcase in a closet. Ahl and the three accomplices were later tried and convicted. This whole affair caused some friction among federal, state and local officials all vying for the right to claim the money, but the federal government ultimately won out.

Born in 1893, Bessie Jones was known for her generosity. She used to donate money to local churches and civic organizations and helped many African American families survive during the Depression. The Internal Revenue Service was not as charitable. Federal agents came after her in 1966 after learning that she had $100,000 stashed away in a safe deposit box and another $90,000 in her checking account. Bessie claimed that she was unaware that management in her profession had to pay income taxes. She pled guilty in 1967 to five counts of tax evasion and was sentenced to one year in federal prison. She served a few months before being released early due to poor health.

"Something Had to Give": The Camp Hill Prison Riots

The ashes fell like snowflakes from a sky thick with the stink of toxic chemicals and ozone from electrical fires. *Sentinel* reporters could see prison inmates warm themselves by the bonfires as the greenhouse and its stock of fertilizer burned in the night. At one point, they could hear the prisoners utter a bloodcurdling cheer as the riot took on a fever pitch. Here and there, giant corkscrews of smoke and jets of flame rose up from the ruins of the State Correctional Institution near Camp Hill in Lower Allen Township. It was the evening of October 26–27, 1989, and all hell had broken loose for the second time in as many days.

The inmates had taken over. They had the advantage. They figured that the police would not rush in while it was still dark, even though fire engines parked both inside and outside the perimeter fence cast some light by way of emergency generators. The prison power supply was knocked out shortly after the second round of rioting had begun. As inmates looted, a small army of law enforcement officers peered through the coils of razor wire at the chaos beyond, content with keeping the uprising contained.

The *Sentinel* reported how inmates raided the prison furniture factory of tools and had used gasoline from lawnmowers to make Molotov cocktails, which set fire to almost anything that could burn. In areas where the inmates had control, firefighters could only stand by and watch the buildings burn to avoid the risk of injury. There was a case where prisoners pelted firefighters with rocks as they tried to battle a fire beyond the main gate. "It's just chaos," said Harry Frey, who was the fire chief of Shiremanstown at the time.

Early in the evening, a fire truck was seen near the southwest corner of the prison attempting to use an aerial ladder to fight a fire just over the fence. About 9:30 p.m., reporters saw a dozen inmates armed with a chainsaw approach the fence in that same area. There was a huge explosion only minutes later as a building a few hundred yards away collapsed. Hours passed before another large explosion tore through the prison compound at about 1:10 a.m., releasing a column of flame into the night sky. That blast was allegedly caused by an inmate throwing an oxygen bottle into a fire.

Between four hundred and five hundred state troopers from six counties reinforced the estimated one hundred local police tasked with holding the inmates to the prison grounds. Two state police helicopters circled above to keep watch as talks began after 10:00 p.m. with inmates who had approached the main gate to initiate negotiations. The prisoners demanded changes in the medical and family visitation rules along with a press conference and amnesty for their actions.

Not all inmates were involved in the riot or negotiations. Several hundred prisoners were seen moving to the corners of the secured compound trying to distance themselves from those responsible for the violence. "We were scared out of our minds to where we were crying, shaking and praying until early morning," an unnamed inmate would later tell the *Sentinel*. He relayed stories of rioters attacking snitches, including one prisoner who was reported as being repeatedly beaten and sodomized. "There is no peace in that prison," a former inmate told the newspaper. "It's like a war every day."

Meanwhile, medical teams worked frantically under spotlights and the cover of trees to treat the injured from both sides, hurt mostly by blunt-force trauma from beatings and makeshift weapons. The reporters compared these men and women to medics in a combat zone. "We just had to separate our emotions and concentrate on the job at hand," said Dave Crossley, township emergency medical service chief. Luckily, Lower Allen had hosted a practice for the county mass casualty team only the month before.

Mounted state police, along with two groups of troopers on foot, marched through the main gate at about midnight. Officers were seen using flex wrap to secure prisoners left sitting around in the yard, but police had to be careful as some inmates used cigarette lighters to burn through the restraints. Despite this, law enforcement soon gained the upper hand, and by 9:30 a.m. October 27 the rioting had ended.

This second of two riots began about 7:00 p.m. the previous evening, less than a day after prison staff had regained control of SCI Camp Hill following seven hours of rioting the day before. Though state police did fire guns to keep inmates away from the perimeter fence, no one had escaped or was killed during the riots. However, more than one hundred people were injured during the two days of riots, including fifty-seven who had to be hospitalized. Sixteen of the thirty-one prison buildings were severely damaged or destroyed during the riots. It took months for the Pennsylvania Department of Corrections to rebuild the fifty-two-acre complex located about four miles west of Harrisburg.

What became SCI Camp Hill opened in 1941 as a juvenile reformatory but was converted in 1976 into a medium-security adult facility. Just before the riots, this prison had a population of 2,607 inmates, or about 781 over its rated capacity of 1,826. This included 230 inmates serving life sentences.

The *Sentinel* reported how residents living within a few miles said that overcrowding was an important factor that contributed to the riots.

Throughout the crisis, the newspaper quoted unnamed sources who had inside knowledge of the situation at the prison. A correctional officer compared SCI Camp Hill to a powder keg ready to blow. "You can't keep shoving people on top of people...Something had to give." He attributed the crisis not just to overcrowding but also to understaffing and too much leniency with prisoners.

Another guard told the *Sentinel* that one reason for the riots was a rumor circulating among the inmates about a proposed reduction in family day visits from three to two days per year and a new rule prohibiting picnic lunches on those family days. Superintendent Robert Freeman disputed these claims by telling journalists that visiting privileges had not been eliminated but instead that a ban was put into place just days before the riots barring food from being brought in by family members. Freeman said this was done to prevent contraband from being slipped into the prison. This touched off complaints from inmates.

The first riot at Camp Hill came only two days after a riot in Huntingdon state prison left nineteen inmates and twenty-nine staff members injured. That riot involved inmates taking over a cellblock and included such behavior as breaking windows, destroying furniture and setting small fires.

Rioting at SCI Camp Hill began at about 3:00 p.m. October 25, when an inmate assaulted a correctional officer at Gatehouse E, which served as a checkpoint within the inside wall. Fighting soon spread to two cellblock areas, the food service area and the prison commissary.

Carl Meiss III was a corporal with the Lower Allen Township police department in October 1989. He was among the one hundred local officers called to the scene of the first riot. His assignment that day was to enter the prison grounds and help to coordinate communications. In a ten-year retrospective, done by the *Sentinel*, Meiss recalled a feeling of absolute frustration at the sight of inmates beating two correctional officers in the prison yard. One of the officers was in a chair blindfolded and handcuffed.

"We could do nothing except report what was happening," said Meiss, who would spend most of that first night juggling three radios as he relayed messages among the various groups working the scene. The local police were reinforced by county sheriff deputies and more than two hundred state troopers from six counties. Three state police helicopters circled the area most of the afternoon and night. Police blockades were deployed at all roads leading to the prison, turning away everyone but nearby residents.

The riot also drew a response from local fire companies and ambulance units including a ladder truck from Mount Holly Springs Citizens Fire

Company. Driver Fred Bomberger recalled the following during an interview with *Sentinel* reporter Julie Franklin:

> *We got down there and the first orders we received were to rescue some staff people off the auditorium roof. I didn't know how long they had been up there...They were in the auditorium doing something and they got up there for the safety of it. As soon as we finished that, we were setting up lighting when the prisoners decided they were going to stone us. They were throwing half bricks over the fence and toward our truck and other apparatus.*

Bomberger counted about twenty-five dents in the company ladder truck. He added that one of the bricks hit a New Cumberland firefighter on the head and that Mount Holly firefighters were among those who attended to the man before he was taken to an ambulance outside the gates. Bomberger goes on to describe the scene further for the newspaper reporter: "There is one section of the prison that they turned into shambles. There was food from the commissary and other stuff scattered through the whole yard. There were windows broken out of everything."

A press conference with Camp Hill prison officials.

The first riot quickly drew the attention of both local and national media. *Sentinel* staffers were among those assigned to the scene around the clock to get the story. Assistant Superintendent John Palakovich refused to answer the barrage of questions fired at him by some reporters: "You don't understand. The inmates are watching the broadcasts...We don't want to give them any more information than we have to. Many inmates have radios and television sets."

Over and over again, Palakovich assured the media that the prison was secure and that the situation posed no threat to the community, but the smoke billowing for hours over the prison was probably unsettling to neighbors. There was even an unconfirmed report that the prison superintendent's son was secured by Penbrook Borough police after stepping off his school bus about a mile from the prison.

By 10:45 p.m., prison officials announced that the entire facility was secure and that the inmates were being returned to their cells. This, however, was only a foretaste of greater mayhem to come. Damage sustained in the first riot set the stage for the second riot, even though SCI Camp Hill was in a complete lockdown with all inmates confined to their cells.

The *Sentinel* reported how the metal covers over several lock control panels were removed during the first riot. Fifteen correctional officers told the Associated Press that they had reported the damage to supervisors and had asked for forty-three locks to secure several doors in the cellblocks but only received nineteen locks.

This oversight allowed the inmates to free themselves during the evening meal by reaching a hand out of their cells and releasing the exposed lever in each control panel. Guards also claimed that prison supervisors ignored reports filed two weeks before the riot quoting inmates warning of coming trouble. As a result of the AP story, Freeman was suspended as the prison superintendent.

The twin riots forced the transfer of many inmates to other state and federal prisons to allow for repairs to SCI Camp Hill. The *Sentinel* reported how on Friday, October 27, the first of nearly eight hundred shackled and handcuffed inmates were moved out in a caravan of ten buses escorted by an equal number of police cruisers. Some prisoners reportedly waved to bystanders outside the prison gates, while others looked angry.

As prison officials worked to identify those responsible for the riots, they kept hundreds of inmates out in the prison yard in leg shackles and handcuffs. This prompted the American Civil Liberties Union to file a federal lawsuit on behalf of four inmates claiming that the continued restraints were designed

The front gate of the Camp Hill prison shortly after the riots.

solely to inflict cruel and unusual punishment. The suit also claimed that inmates lacked adequate clothing, heat, food, plumbing and medical care. Federal judge Sylvia Rambo, a Dickinson School of Law graduate, ordered the restraints removed and the inmates given showers, clean clothes, pillows and mattresses: "Common sense and reason indicate that the longer the inmates are kept restrained, the possibility of future agitation and unrest becomes greater."

Prison officials argued that the restraints were necessary for the safety and security of staff and inmates. But the troubles did not end there. State lawmakers soon launched their own inquiries into what lead to the riots. Governor Robert Casey appointed a three-member commission tasked with investigating the riots and developing an action plan to address overcrowding in state prisons. Casey also announced that the state government would reimburse municipalities and emergency responders for excess costs incurred during the riots.

As for Cumberland County, the state police launched a two-year investigation that resulted in charges being filed against 166 inmates deemed responsible for crimes associated with the twin riots.

BIBLIOGRAPHY

BLOOD FOR BLOOD

"The Greatest Melancholy": The Pontiac War

"Bouquet's Plan of Defense." In *Two Hundred Years in Cumberland County*. Carlisle, PA: Hamilton Library and Historical Association, 1951. Reprinted from the Papers of Colonel Henry Bouquet.

Conrad, W.P. *From Terror to Freedom in the Cumberland Valley*. Greencastle, PA: Lillian S. Besore Memorial Library, 1976.

"Desolation of So Many Families." In *Two Hundred Years in Cumberland County*. Carlisle, PA: Hamilton Library and Historical Association, 1951. Reprinted from the Papers of Colonel Henry Bouquet.

Donehoo, George. *A History of the Cumberland Valley in Pennsylvania*. Harrisburg, PA: Susquehanna History Association, 1930.

"Killing, Scalping and Butchering." In *Two Hundred Years in Cumberland County*. Carlisle, PA: Hamilton Library and Historical Association, 1951. Reprinted from Historical Collections Relating to the American Colonial Church.

"No Respite From Indian Ravages." In *Two Hundred Years in Cumberland County*. Carlisle, PA: Hamilton Library and Historical Association, 1951. Reprinted from Historical Collections Relating to the American Colonial Church.

Pennsylvania Gazette. August 9, 1764, and August 30, 1764.

Wing, Conway, Reverend. *History of Cumberland County.* Philadelphia, PA: Herald Printing Co., 1879.

"A Perfect Holocaust": The Enoch Brown Massacre

Bates, Samuel P., and Jacob Fraise Richard. *History of Franklin County, Pennsylvania.* Chicago: Warner Beerst & Co., 1887. Reprinted Evansville, IN: Unigraphic. Inc., 1975. Sponsored by the Greencastle-Antrim Civil War Roundtable, Greencastle, Pennsylvania.

Donehoo, George. *A History of the Cumberland Valley in Pennsylvania.* Harrisburg, PA: Susquehanna History Association, 1930.

McCauley, I.H. *Historical Sketch of Franklin County, Pennsylvania.* Chambersburg, PA: D.F. Pursal, 1878. Reprinted Evansville, IN: Unigraphic. Inc., 1979. Sponsored by the Print Peddler.

Pennsylvania Gazette. August 9, 1764.

Ruwet, Jane P. "The Enoch Brown Massacre." Lamberton and Hamilton Library Association prize essay. Carlisle, PA, 1962.

SUFFER THE CHILDREN

"The Fierce Indignation of Heaven": Teen Slave Child Killer

Kline's Weekly Gazette. June 10, 1801; June 24, 1801; July 22, 1801.

Lougbridge, Nancy. "Chloe's Story." *Cumberland County History* (Summer 1987).

Wing, Conway, Reverend. *History of Cumberland County.* Philadelphia, PA: Herald Printing Co., 1879.

"What...Fiendish Cause": The Brushtown Tragedy

American Volunteer. "A Horrible Tragedy." June 6, 1883.

Carlisle Herald. "A Horrible Crime." June 7, 1883.

Daily Evening Sentinel. "The Brushtown Tragedy." June 2, 1883.

———. "A Horrible Murder and Suicide." June 1, 1883.

———. "The Victims Buried." June 3, 1883.

"A Soft Tish, Tish, Tish": The Babes in the Woods Mystery

Evening Sentinel. "All 5 Tragedy Victims Identified; Love Affair Seen as Motive." November 30, 1934.

———. "Case Now Closed to State Police." December 1, 1934.

———. "Children Mourn Tragedy Victims." November 28, 1934.

———. "Children's Identity and Cause of Death Remain Unknown." November 27, 1934.

———. "Crowds at Graves of Three Girls." December 3, 1934.

———. "Feud in Family of Babes Relatives." November 1934.

———. "Mountain Tragedy Stirs Whole Nation." November 26, 1934.

———. "Mystery Solved." November 30, 1934.

———. "Psychologist Gives Theory in 3 Deaths." November 28, 1934.

———. "Solution Nearer in Girls' Deaths." November 26, 1934.

———. "10,000 View Babes Found Dead in Mountain." November 26, 1934.

———. "3 Girls Found Dead in Mountain." November 24, 1934.

———. "Three Girls Identified as Members of Tourist Family; Couple Slain at Altoona Believed Their Companions." November 28, 1934.

———. "3 Girls to Have Legion Burial." November 27, 1934.

———. "3 Sisters, Victims of Mountain Tragedy Are Laid to Rest." December 1, 1934.

———. "To the Memory of Three Little Girls (a poem)." November 30, 1934.

———. "Woodsman Tells of Finding Bodies." November 26, 1934.

Finch, John. "The Case of the Babes in the Woods." *Patriot,* November 24, 1974.

Wylie, Dorothy. "This Is the Story of the Tragedy of the 'Babes in the Woods.'" *Evening Sentinel,* November 22, 1974.

GALLOWS GROUND

A Most Dastardly Pursuit: The Murder of David Musselman

Carlisle Gazette. May 16, 1787, and June 13, 1787.

"Murder on the Highway." In *Two Hundred Years in Cumberland County.* Carlisle, PA: Hamilton Library and Historical Association, 1951. Reprinted from the *Carlisle Gazette,* January 10, 1787.

Podvia, Mark. "Early Criminal Justice." In *Cumberland Justice: Legal Practice in Cumberland County, 1750 to 2000*. Carlisle, PA: Cumberland County Bar Foundation, 2001.

Wing, Conway, Reverend. *History of Cumberland County*. Philadelphia, PA: Herald Printing Co., 1879.

"Hell's Fire Fury": The Execution of Ed Donnelly

American Volunteer. "Local History: Executions Years Ago." July 7, 1923.

"The Donally Execution." In *Two Hundred Years in Cumberland County*. Carlisle, PA: Hamilton Library and Historical Association, 1951. Reprinted from the *Cumberland Register*, August 18, 1807; November 10, 1807; January 12, 1808; February 2, 1808; and February 9, 1808.

Kline's Carlisle Weekly Gazette. "Confession of Edward Donnelly." February 12, 1808.

———. November 13, 1807; January 15, 1808; February 5, 1808; February 12, 1808.

———. "The Students Adventure." February 12, 1808.

Podvia, Mark. "The Trial of Edward Donally." In *Cumberland Justice: Legal Practice in Cumberland County, 1750 to 2000*. Carlisle, PA: Cumberland County Bar Foundation, 2001.

Wing, Conway, Reverend. *History of Cumberland County*. Philadelphia, PA: Herald Printing Co., 1879.

"A Life for a Life": The People v. Charles Salyards

Burgess, Fred. "Police Officers Rare in 19th Century." *Sentinel*, February 25, 1989.

Carlisle Evening Sentinel. "Almost Mobbed." April 12, 1893.

———. "Carlisle's Murder." April 10, 1893.

———. "The Case Against Salyards." May 20, 1893.

———. "The Case in the Hands of the Jury." May 26, 1893.

———. "Charles Salyards." November 15, 1893.

———. "Doesn't Like Hanging." December 9, 1893.

———. "Friday Morning: The Second Day of the Murder Trial." May 19, 1893.

———. "A Letter From the Jail." July 29, 1893.

———. "The Martin Murder." April 11, 1893.

———. "The Murder Trial." May 23, 1893.

———. "Must Hang." February 10, 1894.

———. "A New Trial Asked." June 7, 1893.

———. "The Pardon Refused." January 5, 1894.

———. "Practically An Unbroken Chain of Evidence." May 24, 1893.

———. "Salyards Attempts Suicide." February 28, 1894.

———. "The Salyards Case." April 17, 1893.

———. "The Salyards Case." January 15, 1894.

———. "The Salyards Case." July 3, 1893.

———. "The Salyards Case: The Arguments on the Motion for a New Trial." July 5, 1893.

———. "The Salyards Case: The Arguments on the Motion for a New Trial." July 6, 1893.

———. "Salyards: Doom Sealed." November 15, 1893.

———. "Salyards In Court." May 15, 1893.

———. "The Salyards Letter." March 8, 1894.

———. "Salyards Must Hang." January 5, 1894.

———. "Salyards On Trial." May 22, 1893.

———. "Salyards' Record." April 13, 1893.

———. "Salyards: Sentenced to be Hanged." July 15, 1893.

———. "Some of the Evidence Filed in the Salyards Case." January 16, 1894.

———. "True Charity." April 12, 1893.

———. "What of Salyards?" July 14, 1893.

Carlisle Weekly Herald. "Salyards Hanged." March 1, 1894.

Podvia, Mark. "The Salyards Murder Trial." In *Cumberland Justice: Legal Practice in Cumberland County, 1750 to 2000.* Carlisle, PA: Cumberland County Bar Foundation, 2001.

HELL STREET BLUES

"Peace to His Ashes": The McNamara Murder

American Volunteer. "Confession of Perrier, the Murderer." September 2, 1858.

———. "Horrible Affair: Murder Upon the Street." June 10, 1858.

———. "Military Funeral." June 10, 1858.

Carlisle Herald. "Murder." June 9, 1858.

———. "Proceedings in Court." September 1, 1858.

"No Earthly Tribunal": The Gambler Who Wagered the Truth

Hoch, Paul D. *Carlisle History and Lore: It's People, Places and Stories Carlisle.* Carlisle, PA: Cumberland County Historical Society, 2003.

Podvia, Mark. "The Foulk Murder Trial." In *Cumberland Justice: Legal Practice in Cumberland County, 1750 to 2000.* Carlisle, PA: Cumberland County Bar Foundation, 2001.

Thompson, D.W. *Carlisle Outlaw: The Life and Times of Charley Foulk 1837–1884.* Carlisle, PA: Thompson's Book Store, 1975.

"The Advent of Thieves": Tensions with the Military

Burgess, Fred. "Police Officers Rare in 19th Century." *Sentinel*, February 25, 1989.

Carlisle Herald. "An Attempt at Riot." October 12, 1860.

Donavin, S.K. "The Invasion: Rebel Occupancy of Carlisle, 1863." *Cumberland County History* (Summer 1998).

Kennedy, Kenneth Wade, Jr. "Tensions of the Civil War Era." Lamberton and Hamilton Library Association prize essay. Carlisle, PA, 1962.

Thompson, D.W. *Carlisle Outlaw: The Life and Times of Charley Foulk 1837–1884.* Carlisle, PA: Thompson's Book Store, 1975.

Tousey, Thomas G. *Military History of Carlisle and Carlisle Barracks.* Richmond, VA: Dietz Press, 1939.

"Scene of Terror and Confusion": The Riot of 1867

Kennedy, Kenneth Wade, Jr. "Tensions of the Civil War Era." Lamberton and Hamilton Library Association prize essay, 1962.

Star of the Valley. "Riot in Carlisle." March 23, 1867.

"A Street Battle." In *Two Hundred Years in Cumberland County.* Carlisle, PA: Hamilton Library and Historical Association, 1951. Reprinted from the *American Volunteer*, March 21, 1867.

Thompson, D.W. *Carlisle Outlaw: The Life and Times of Charley Foulk 1837–1884.* Carlisle, PA: Thompson's Book Store, 1975.

Tousey, Thomas G. *Military History of Carlisle and Carlisle Barracks.* Richmond, VA: Dietz Press, 1939.

A Taste of Malice

The Bitter Bread of Jealousy: The Case of Sarah Clark

Mader, Sandy. "Women of Carlisle's East End." *Cumberland County History* (Summer/Winter 2003).

Morefield, Mary Anne. "Arsenic in the Leaven." *Cumberland County History* (Summer 1988).

Podvia, Mark. "The Murder Trial of Sarah Clark." In *Cumberland Justice: Legal Practice in Cumberland County, 1750 to 2000.* Carlisle, PA: Cumberland County Bar Foundation, 2001.

Wing, Conway, Reverend. *History of Cumberland County.* Philadelphia, PA: Herald Printing Co., 1879.

"Political Clarification": The Case Against Paul Schoeppe

Carlisle Herald. "The Schoeppe Murder Trial." June 11, 1869.

———. "The Schoeppe Murder Trial." June 4, 1869.

———. "The Schoeppe Murder Trial." May 28, 1869.

———. "The Steinnecke Will Case." February 19, 1869.

———. "The Steinnecke Will Case." February 26, 1869.

Podvia, Mark. "The Trial of Dr. Paul Schoeppe." In *Cumberland Justice: Legal Practice in Cumberland County, 1750 to 2000.* Carlisle, PA: Cumberland County Bar Foundation, 2001.

Wing, Conway, Reverend. *History of Cumberland County.* Philadelphia, PA: Herald Printing Co., 1879.

"Cruel and Fatal Work": The Death of Mary Kiehl

Valley Sentinel. "Found Guilty: The Kiehl Murder Case." November 21, 1879.

———. "The Kiehl Case." July 25, 1879.

———. "The Kiehl Poisoning Case." September 26, 1879.

———. "Mrs. Catherine Zell Saved From The Gallows." February 27, 1880.

———. "A New Trial Refused." December 19, 1879.

———. "The Wynkoop Case: A Trial of Great Interest." January 23, 1880.

"A Struggle for Supremacy": The Candy Man Cadaver

Burgess, Fred. "The Sensation of 1909." *Sentinel*, September 2, 2007.
Evening Sentinel. "Angelo Tornatore and Mrs. Pishotta Each Found 'Not Guilty.'" September 28, 1909.
———. "Body of John Pishotta Buried This Morning." April 16, 1909.
———. "Coroner's Jury Holds Inquest in Pishotta Murder Case." April 14, 1909.
———. "Coroner's Jury in Pishotta Murder Case Renders Verdict." April 15, 1909.
———. "Defendants in Pishotta Murder Case Granted Separate Trials." September 16, 1909.
. "A Foul Murder Committed." April 13, 1909.
———. "Good Progress in Pishotta Case Made Today." September 18, 1909.
———. "Jury in Murder Case Finally Selected." September 17, 1909.
———. "Killed Pishotta in Self Defense Is Tornatore's Plea." September 20, 1909.
———. "Tornatore on Witness Stands Tells in Detail How He Killed Pishotta." September 21, 1909.
Meehan, Susan E. "A Murder in the James Hamilton House." *Cumberland County History* (Winter 2007).

COLD CASES AND TRIALS BY FIRE

"Lead Kindly Light": The Moonshine Murders

Evening Sentinel. "Double Murder." May 17, 1924.
———. "Lamb's Gap Murder Still a Mystery." May 22, 1924.
———. "May Take Years to Solve Murder." May 23, 1924.
———. "Murder of Two Remains Unsolved." May 19, 1924.
———. "No Light Thrown on Double Murder." May 26, 1924.
———. "State Police Are Hunting Murderer." May 20, 1924.
———. "State Police Still Follow Trails." May 21, 1924.

"Magic Ball and Triggerman": The Courtroom Slaying of 1955

Evening Sentinel. "Court Shooting Probe Urged." United Press International, August 3, 1955.

———. "Haines Defense Ends." September 27, 1955.

———. "Haines Goes on Trial For Life Here Tomorrow." September 20, 1955.

———. "Haines Held for Grand Jury." August 5, 1955.

———. "Haines Held on Murder Charge." August 3, 1955.

———. "Haines Is Indicted on Murder Charge in Court Shooting." September 12, 1955.

———. "Haines Is Sent to PA Prison in Philadelphia." September 27, 1955.

———. "Haines Knocks Himself Out." August 12, 1955.

———. "Haines Makes Quick Entrance into Half-Filled Court Room." September 21, 1955.

———. "John D. Faller Eulogized by County Association." August 6, 1955.

———. "John D. Faller, Jr." August 3, 1955.

———. "John D. Faller Rites Saturday." August 3, 1955.

———. "John D. Faller Slain, 3 Others Shot in Court." August 2, 1955.

———. "Life Term for Haines." September 28, 1955.

———. "Not Guilty Plea Is Entered by Haines in Court Shooting." September 15, 1955.

———. "Psychiatrist Says Haines Was Conscious of Action in Court Room Shooting." September 26, 1955.

———. "Second Courtroom Shooting in Penna." August 3, 1955.

———. "Terrible Tragedy Here." August 4, 1955.

———. "Testimony Starts In Haines' Trial; Top Penalty Asked." September 23, 1955.

———. "Three Jurors Are Selected as Trial for Haines Opens." September 21, 1955.

———. "Trial for Haines in Court Shooting Set for Sept. 21." September 3, 1955.

———. "Weidner Will Ask for Death Penalty in Court Shooting." September 16, 1955.

———. "Weidner Will Seek Sept. Trial for Man Accused in Courtroom Shooting." August 4, 1955.

Faller, George B., Jr. "Tragedy." *Cumberland Justice: Legal Practice in Cumberland County, 1750 to 2000.* Carlisle, PA: Cumberland County Bar Foundation, 2001.

Sentinel. "Senators Grill Top Prison Official." Associated Press, November 1, 1989.

"Blood on Their Hands": The Murdered Madam

Amerson, Carman. "Bessie's Case Still Open." *Sentinel*, February 24, 1990.

Amerson, Carman, and Richard Reitz. "Lawyer Holding Bessie's Sex Book." *Sentinel*, June 28, 1990.

Evening Sentinel. "Escape Attempt Foiled." October 18, 1972.

———. "Woman Held in Bessie Jones' Murder." October 2, 1972.

Jones, Ray. "Woman Accused in Jones Murder Held for Court." *Evening Sentinel*, October 25, 1972.

Kahn, Harold. "Bessie Jones Case: Witness Cites Robbery Try." *Evening Sentinel*, February 13, 1973.

———. "Jury Gets Murder Case; Syndicate Claim Hit." *Evening Sentinel*, February 14, 1973.

———. "Suspect Acquitted." *Evening Sentinel*, February 15, 1973.

Mader, Sandy. "Women of Carlisle's East End." *Cumberland County History* (Summer/Winter 2003).

Trout, Leslie. "Woman Arraigned in Miss Jones' Death." *Evening Sentinel*, October 3, 1972.

"Something Had to Give": The Camp Hill Prison Riots

Amerson, Carman, Hugh Bronstein and Dan Miller. "Camp Hill Prison Riot Quelled." *Sentinel*, October 26, 1989.

———. "Surrender Ends Night of Violence." *Sentinel*, October 27, 1989.

Amerson, Carman, and Dan Miller. "42 Injured Before Police Crush Prison Riot." *Sentinel*, October 26, 1989.

Bronstein, Hugh. "Guard: Prison 'A Powder Keg.'" *Sentinel*, October 26, 1989.

Bronstein, Hugh, and Dan Miller. "Guard Believes Inside 'Just About Destroyed.'" *Sentinel*, October 27, 1989.

Carver, Julie. "County May Take Up to 24 Inmates." *Sentinel*, October 27, 1989.

Franklin, Julie. "Camp Hill Still 33 Percent Overcrowded." *Sentinel*, November 4, 1989.

———. "County Prison Uprising Quashed." *Sentinel*, October 30, 1989.

———. "County Tallies Riot Costs." *Sentinel*, November 1, 1989.

———. "Mt. Holly Describes Scene Inside Wall." *Sentinel*, October 26, 1989.

————. "Visitor: Prison 'A Wasteland.'" *Sentinel*, November 4, 1989.

Franklin, Julie, and Mark Weinberg. "Caravans Head to Crowded State Prisons." *Sentinel*, October 28, 1989.

Henshaw, Steven. "County to Ask State to Repay Costs." *Sentinel*, October 28, 1989.

————. "'Just Plain Chaos.'" *Sentinel*, October 27, 1989.

Henshaw, Steven, and Mark Weinberg. "Senators: Build Jails." *Sentinel*, October 30, 1989.

Lindt, Susan. "Prison Riot: 'We Were Scared Out of Our Minds.'" *Sentinel*, October 24, 1999.

Long, Barbara Phillips. "Not to Be Forgotten: Lower Allen Officers on the Front Lines." *Sentinel*, October 24. 1999.

Patriot. "Last Inmate Plead Guilty to Prison Riot." November 5, 1991.

Sentinel. "ACLU May Sue Prison." Associated Press, November 4, 1989.

————. "Camp Hill Prison Riot Timeline." Associated Press, October 24, 1999.

————. "Senators Grill Top Prison Official." Associated Press, November 1, 1989.

————. "Suit Says Inmates Mistreated." Associated Press, November 7, 1989.

————. "Top Official Suspends Prison Superintendent." Associated Press, November 2, 1989.

ABOUT THE AUTHOR

Joseph David Cress is an award-winning journalist with almost twenty years of full-time newspaper experience. For eleven years, he has worked as a staff reporter with the *Sentinel* in Carlisle. His first book, *Remembering Carlisle: Tales from the Cumberland Valley*, was released in November 2009. *Murder & Mayhem in Cumberland County* is his second book with The History Press. Cress lives in York, Pennsylvania, with his wife Stacey, dogs Dottie and Rosco and cats Chewie and Boone.

Courtesy of the Sentinel.

Visit us at
www.historypress.net

www.ingramcontent.com/pod-product-compliance
Lightning Source LLC
Chambersburg PA
CBHW070349100426
42812CB00005B/1468